I0423117

How to analyze people

Become a master of the human mind. Learn to read body language and influence people in five minutes with speed reading, the art of manipulation and dark psychology

Ryan Carter

Table of Contents

Introduction

Congratulations on downloading *How to Analyze People* and thank you for doing so.

The following chapters will discuss:

How to learn to read body language and influence people in five minutes with speed reading, the art of manipulation and dark psychology.

There are plenty of books on this subject on the market, thanks again for choosing this one! Every effort was made to ensure it is full of as much useful information as possible, please enjoy!

Body Language and Facial Expressions, together they form what I call Non-Verbal Intelligence. It is something that fascinates most, but I still wonder, what is it? Why do I need it? How does this change my life?

Where and how you can make use of Nonverbal Intelligence, many people still have questions about the topic.

Do I really need this? Why learn? What do I get out of it? Will it change my life in what? But I do not even want to be a professional in the field.

Well, you just do not know yet or did not realize what you are missing out on not knowing about Body Language.

Non-Verbal Intelligence in Your Life

Well, let's first follow the principle that you do not live in a bubble, isolated from the rest of the world. Based on this principle, you live with other people, relate, buy, sell, speak, and communicate. Body Language is about people, so if you are a human, this is the first reason you should learn about it.

Technologies are made to give human beings more quality of life, social networks are for humans, so if everything is done for us, we need to understand that it's all about providing more quality of life for us.

In Your Marriage Relationship

You may not be married, but you have a loving or even casual relationship. You know that poor communication is what triggers the biggest problems in a relationship.

How much would your marital life improve? If you could recognize through Micro facial expressions and body language your partner's emotions and intentions? Would that improve your life?

Know the signs of interest of your partner, as well as perceive signs that there is something wrong.

Sometimes, we imagine things where they do not exist, because we distrust based on our instinct. If we know how to read the other person, we can see when our suspicions are only the fruit of our imagination, as well as whether this image has any background of truth.

The most reliable source for detecting lies (emotional incongruities) is through our body. Our Body Language makes great revelations about what we want to hide.

I have had testimony from both sides: People who saw that it was all a question of unfounded mistrust, of their spouses, both men and women, as well as of wives and husbands who did not know they were deceived and came to discover extramarital relationships, after participating in a training.

In Relationship with Your Children

Children never grow up, that's what most parents think. Concern changes according to the phases of life, but they will never be completely absent.

The most worrying phase for the vast majority of parents is adolescence. Where he goes, who he goes with, what time he returns, and we know that the answers may not always be the sincerest, because the children are afraid of being scolded.

Through Non-Verbal Intelligence, it is possible to analyze behaviors, detect the emotions and signs of congruencies, through Micro Facial Expressions and Body Language.

Many parents only realize that there is something wrong with their children when they are already involved more deeply in situations that could be perceived before.

Adolescence is often a reflection of childhood. Children who suffer abuse tend to repress some information out of fear and in adolescence end up giving away what has been kept for a long time.

Parents should know how to read their children's emotions and how to detect when there is something wrong.

We all know people who are brilliant professionals in their areas of practice, have developed all theory, understand everything from content, but do not know how to deal with people. And how important are people at that point?

Imagine a teacher who knows everything about a subject in which you have learning difficulties. If the teacher is good and knows how to pass the content, you are interested in learning about it. If he is the type that knows everything but does not know how to pass the content, you soon dislike him.

Many professionals with a high intellectual capacity no longer grow in their careers because they are only concerned with the logical and theoretical part when in reality, they should be focused on developing the art of "making friends and influencing people."

People open doors, and their knowledge and intellectual ability help you stay on these opportunities that appear.

Verbal Intelligence is an intelligence that you can and should develop. Your perception of people will increase in order to become differentiated in what you already do.

Each person has their way of acting, their gestures, and common traits. Some traits, however, are related to your personality and are useful in identifying what we can expect from them.

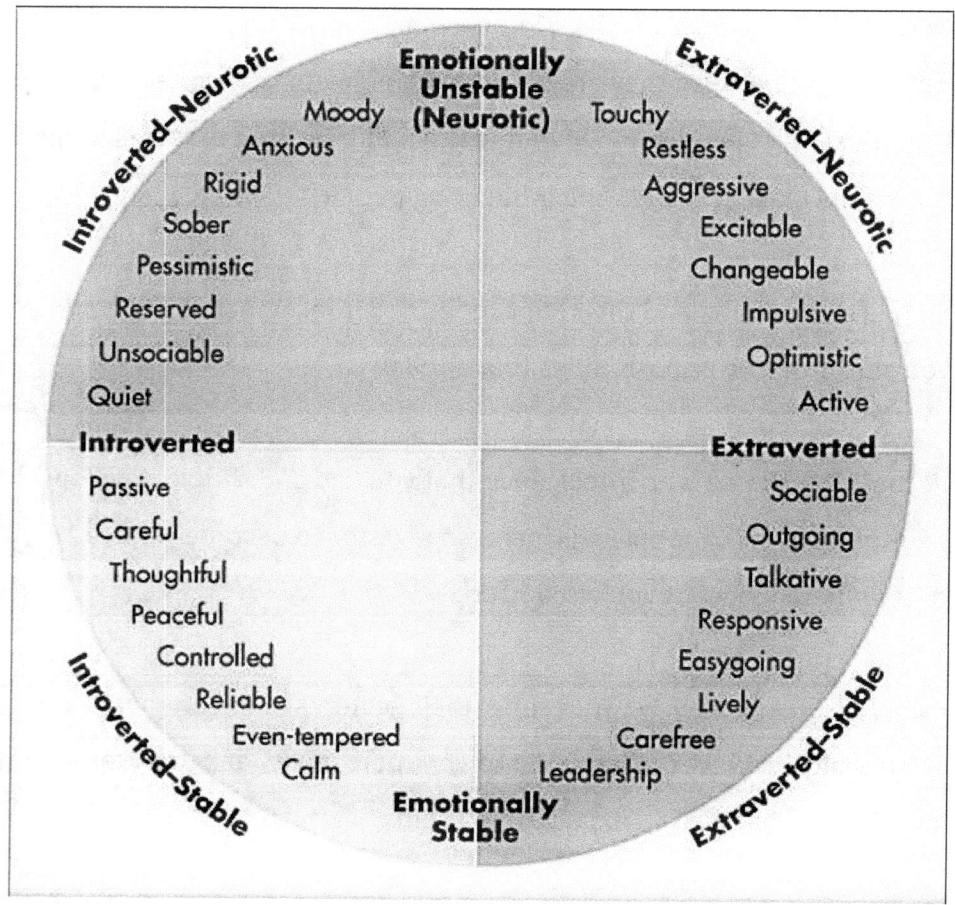

Step 1: The Details

First, you need to realize what is or is not a natural persona of the person. Some gestures like wiggling the leg in a standby situation or looking at the ceiling may be common characteristics. However, when such actions happen at a specific time, you can identify what causes them. These behaviors may show, among other things, disappointment, anger, or anxiety.

Creating a "database" of the gestures that the person performs in their day to day life will help you to know when something is not right. What escapes from the pattern indicates an abnormality. Looking at the inconsistencies then becomes the next step.

Step 2: The Interpretation

In identifying gestures that are not common, we must understand the situation in which they appear, remembering that they are generally involuntary. Pay careful attention to the differences that exist between the basis of the data you have created of the person and the gestures in each situation. Remember that they do not perform them to let you know how they feel. They exist.

One example is you notice that a colleague will clear his throat whenever he is nervous. Suddenly, as you introduce some changes in a project, he does so. Something could be wrong.

Comparing the situations and the characteristics equivalent to them allows us to create a new basis, with the abnormalities of the person.

This will be useful, for example, if you need to give news or propose new business ideas. If the person is nervous or shows signs of uncertainty, the attention needs to be redoubled. Another issue concerning abnormal gestures is to see if they happen concomitantly.

Step 3: Recognition

The so-called mirror neurons cause our bodies to reflect the actions of people around us. A smile activates the muscles that make us smile, for example. If you raise your shoulder in concern, it will also alert you.

When we meet someone we like, our facial muscles relax, and our eyebrows are arched. If the caller does not act in the same way, he may be sending you a message: he or she does not like you or is not happy with your actions.

Step 4: Identification

We are often conditioned to look directly at the head of an industry when in a meeting. This person, however, is not necessarily someone that brings best results. The leader may not have a strong personality. Try to find who does.

At a meeting table, the most confident person will probably be the most powerful. To identify them, look for the one who has the most influential voice, an expansive stance, and a broad smile. If you are presenting an idea, identify the most influential voice and your chances of succeeding increase.

On the other hand, some people clearly show signs of lack of confidence. They keep their heads low and do not seem at ease in the environment. Identifying the lack of trust in someone needs to be taken to bring that person back into the process, making them believe more in themselves. One option is to direct questions to them that make them talk more during a meeting, motivating them to put their ideas on the table.

We can still use their words to understand the way they act. The term "decided," for example, indicates that the subject was previously thought and that a decision was not a random choice. The key words of each sentence are that they allow such an understanding of others.

Step 5: The Complete Questionnaire

Each of us has a personality, but you can ask yourself some basic questions to better understand someone's attitudes. The options presented are:

- Is this person introverted or extroverted?
- Does this person attach much importance to your relationship with others?
- How does this person deal with risks and uncertainties?
- What feeds the ego of this person?
- What is this person's behavior when stressed?
- What is this person's behavior when relaxed?

Read the book to understand more about this.

Chapter 1 - Basis of body language

If you want to make sure you know what a person feels just by looking at her face, maybe it's time to understand a little more about body reading, which is nothing more than to realize that gestures and positions also have a lot to say - much more than you can imagine.

To give you an idea, 55% of the information a person relays when communicating comes from body language. This body reading thing is so curious that it is interesting to highlight some of the many types of research already done addressing the theme:

Did you know, for example, that psychopaths can detect vulnerability only by analyzing the way a person walks?

Another study suggests that it is possible to understand what a politician thinks about a particular subject solely based on his hands. Possible?

How To "Read" Someone

Typically, you are wondering how one person interprets the other through body language. You must be aware of the unconscious signals issued by your interlocutor, without them knowing that they are being analyzed. The three key points of body language are:

Speech and Behavior: To tell if a person feels emotionally attuned to you, notice if they use the same words as you; they speak in a tone and at a speed similar to the ones you use to talk; if they are sitting in the same position as you. If the conversation continues at a pace that makes it sound like a "follow the master" game, the emotional connection between both of you is adequately established;

Levels of agitation and activity: If the person does not move, he or she has little interest in what you have to say however if they run out after the meeting, it indicates that they are excited. Several surveys have already confirmed that when a woman swings her feet while on a romantic date, she probably likes the man she is with.

Emphasis and timing: The term "timing" means that the person is speaking or doing the right thing at the right time. If in addition to having a schedule for the relevant comments, the person emphasizes specific points, it means that they are focused and controlled. On the other hand, a person that does not show security in what he speaks, due to lack of timing and emphasis, is easily manipulated.

Still, on the quest for excellence in body language, you need to pay close attention to the interlocutor. In that sense, there are biases that you must analyze to improve your ability to perceive:

Think of the context: Would people in this situation act in the same way that the person who is talking to you is acting?

Look for joint, non-isolated actions: Do not focus on just one detail or gesture. Always observe the entire body.

Compare: How Does This Person Act Normally?

Know that your prejudices can deceive you. To understand the other, you need to understand yourself: see if you are not drawing conclusions because you like or because you do not like the person.

The way the human body communicates is often the subject of research, and scientists have come up with some rather curious specific conclusions about body language:

Crossed legs are a bad sign during negotiations. It sounds bizarre, but business meetings end better when no one is cross-legged. Just to give you an idea, the analysis of 2,000 meetings showed that none of them ended well when at least one person was cross-legged.

Want to know if someone is lying or betraying your trust? Notice that during a conversation the person has these four attitudes: he leans on his hand, he leans on his face, he crosses his arms and he maintains a posture that is tilted somewhere, not erect. These isolated signs do not amount to much, but when presented together, they probably indicate lies and/or betrayal;

On the other hand, research has already proven that trustworthy people are emotionally expressive. Trust someone who is pleasing to all people, and not just to a specific group.

Concerning the hands: Gestures made with the palms down indicate power and the opposite is submission.

Men and women use different body languages at the time of seduction. Women start smiling, raising their eyebrows, lowering their eyelids quickly, and then look away. Next, almost without exception, they place their hands close to their mouths and smile or lick their lips.

Men, on the other hand, inflame the chest, jut their chin, arch their backs, make gestures with their hands and arms and make movements that can demonstrate confidence and call attention to their power.

The fact is that if you want to read the body language, you need to avoid falling into some common traps, after all, crossed arms do not always mean lack of interest. Here are a few common mistakes made by people trying to gauge how others communicate by gesture:

You cannot ignore the context: The idea that someone is with crossed arms does not mean that he or she is not interested. It could be that they are in an icy environment or if the chair in which he or she is sitting does not have an armrest.

Notice the entire picture: Some people become obsessed with the idea of body reading and end up focusing only on one point of analysis, when, in fact, the ideal scenario would be to observe the entire situation: if the person is sweating, how is the breath, if they touch their face and so on;

Realize standard behaviors: If a person is always bouncing, you do not need to analyze it. Now if the person is always bouncing and, from one moment to another, the behavior changes, then you need to pay attention;

Stay tuned for these details: just know that if you already like or dislike a person, it will affect the judgment you make of them. If the person compliments you or if you find her attractive, maybe your judgments about them are favorable, even if you do not realize it - things of the human unconscious.

So, did you already know that body language may end up revealing some information that we do not make clear through words?

Body Language and Non-Verbal Communication

Body language can reveal as much or more about a person than words. Nonverbal behavior works like cookies on the internet: without realizing it, our body constantly transmits sensitive information about our intentions, feelings, and personality. Even when we are still or silent, gestures, postures, facial expressions and appearance speak for us and can be very eloquent.

Body language tells who we are, how we feel or what our tastes are. In the interaction, the nonverbal behavior also informs our degree of understanding and level of agreement, and can even deny what we are saying at that moment.

Unfortunately, in real life it does not happen as on the screen of our browser: no alert message reminds us that cookies will take advantage of any oversight to deliver valuable information about us, something that will inevitably affect the way we relate to others. And even if we were warned, we would probably act as we do when surfing the web: we would ignore cookies and continue looking for the next website. Big mistake.

Speaking is much more than gathering words in a more or less fortunate way; listening is much more than hearing, and communicating is much more than sending and receiving data packets. To communicate is to share rational and emotional information, agreeing with the other person on its meaning and value. And that is not fully achieved without the intervention of nonverbal behavior.

Speaking and body language accompanies us long before we become humans, is strongly linked to the emotional, intuitive and instinctive part of our brain, and develops mainly on the unconscious plane.

Perhaps our species is not more than 200,000 years old, but the origin of our body language dates back to the appearance of the first mammals, about 300 million years ago. The age difference is abysmal. And although the arrogance of our brand-new neo-cortex invites us to think that nonverbal behavior is the most primitive part of communication, in reality, it is that which accumulates the most evolutionary experience and, in all probability, the most influential in our behavior.

Tips to Improve Your Non-Verbal Communication

These practical tips are the first step to become aware of your body language and improve your way of communicating with others.
The instinct and emotions are faithful friends since long before the reason was born. As intelligent and rational as we are, the truth is that nonverbal behavior, emotions, and the unconscious handle our way of communicating at will and go around telling everything about us.

Who Are the Best Non-Verbal Communicators?

Precisely for this reason, the best non-verbal communicators are those who are aware of their body language, people capable of monitoring their behavior and of calibrating the effect it produces on others. There is no exact profile scientifically established, although they are usually observers, with a broad perspective, and open to new experiences and realities. Traits such as emotional stability and empathy also help.

It may be easier to recognize them in the world of art and communication, but they are equally common in all professions. Some studies show that the most influential and persuasive people have a great awareness of their own and other people's body language, regardless of the professional field in which they have triumphed. It is a fundamental condition for success.

Becoming a good nonverbal communicator requires, therefore, developing self-awareness of body behavior, in the same way, that elite athletes perfect the condition of their muscles. The good news is that both skills can be developed with training. In addition, we can do it on our own, and at any time and circumstance.

It's a matter of concentration and to focus attention on the main channels of body language, seeking its congruence and synchronicity with words.

The 7 Channels of Body Language

Nonverbal behavior is expressed mainly through seven channels that, together with verbal discourse, makeup communication.

Facial Expressions: Facial expressions are the most powerful emotional indicator and the first thing we focus our attention to when interacting. Within fractions of a second, our emotional brain decides at its own risk whether a face is likable or not, a process in which reason does not intervene initially, and in which there is no time to utter a single word. In the face, the seven basic emotions are reflected in an innate and universal way: joy, surprise, sadness, fear, anger, disgust, and contempt. Each one has its own code. Learn to distinguish them, essential to master body language.

Gestures: The gestures have a high cultural component, although the latest lines of research also investigate the genetic origin of some gestures, such as expressions of pride, triumph, and power.

Posture: The body posture expresses a degree of interest and openness towards people, reflected in the exposure and in the orientation of the torso. Visually, the position also has a great impact on our personal image, especially to convey confidence, stability, and security.

Appearance: Appearance continues to be one of the most influential channels of communication, despite social advances and the normative effort in the fight for equality. The appearance of a person tells us about their age, sex, origin, culture, profession, or social and economic condition, among many other data. As much as we try to avoid stereotypes, appearance is still the main source of information when forming the first impression of someone. And you know, there is not a second chance to make a good first impression. Some studies also credit the influence of appearance on persuasions, such as the uniform in the security forces or the white coat in the case of doctors.

Haptic: Haptic defines the scientific study of touch and its influence on the way we relate. Touch is essential when establishing intimacy, denotes commitment, and reveals very sensitive information, such as the position of the domain in the interaction. Recent research shows, even, the power of touch when influencing the behavior of others, as occurs between doctors and patients. Physical contact has a marked cultural component: in Latin and Arab countries it is much greater, for example, than in North America or Japan. A brief and light touch in "uncommitted" areas of the body (arms, shoulders and upper back) can be definitive to establish a good relationship.

Proxemics: It is the most direct channel of body language at the time of coming close or going distant. Proxemics has its origin in anthropology and informs us of the use of space in interaction. Some authors divide the distance between individuals in intimate (-45 cms), personal (between 45 cms and 120 cms), social (+120 cms) and public (+360 cms), depending on the type of relationship. The truth is that each person has their own space, and can also vary according to their mood or environmental circumstances. The important thing is two things:

1st - The simplest way to show us close is to physically approach our interlocutor;

2nd - We must pay close attention to any sign of discomfort generated by our approach.

Paralanguage: Voice can say much more than words. Paralanguage is the most reliable emotional indicator, along with facial expressions. The volume, tore or speed of our voice reveals important information, especially when we try to hide our emotions. It often happens to us, for example, when talking on the phone with very close people: it is enough to lister to their tone when answering to know that something is not right. The voice also has a huge influence on credibility and persuasion: nasal voices, high pitched tones, and high volumes have less credit in public. And remember: silence also communicates.

Other channels such as chronémica and oculésica specialize in the value that time and eyes have in non-verbal communication, although both are characterized by their transversal nature and are present in most of the seven main channels.

The Seven Utilities of Body Language

The influence of non-verbal behavior on human interaction is indisputable. The domain of body language is especially useful in some functions of socialization. These are just some:

- Communicate our identity.

- Inform about our ability to relate.

- Achieve precision and understanding.

- Manage the interaction.

- Transmit emotions and feelings.

- Influence others and ourselves.

- Produce deceit.

The 7 Main Areas of Application of Body Language

The mastery of nonverbal behavior techniques has application in all areas of knowledge, and in any area of private and professional life. Hence the growing interest that arises in the correct use of body language. These are just some of the areas of application, in which it is especially effective:

- Communication and personal relationships.

- Teaching and training.

- Sanity and therapy.

- Security and forensic techniques.

- Negotiation and conflict resolution.

- Marketing and customer service.

- Human resources and personnel selection.

We cannot know what a person thinks through their non-verbal behavior, but body language allows us to infer how they feel, what features dominate their personality or what their intentions are, information that is sometimes much more valuable than words. As with verbal communication, we must be very precise in the expression of our own body language and flexible in the interpretation of others.

Chapter 2 - How to Understand Yourself

Sometimes sitting down to do a complete analysis of ourselves is complicated. However, it is an exercise that we must do at least once a month to know what we can improve and how to improve each day.

The daily activity of our life requires analysis, which allows us to perceive in retrospect the positive and negative consequences of our actions. The good news is that today you will learn to do it, so you can see where it is best to improve.
Analyze Yourself and Improve Little by Little!

It is necessary that as women we are aware of our lives and see the good or the bad that we have done and what consequences it has brought us.

The analysis and the daily reflection are processes that commonly must be carried out by us after each activity, action, and the decision was taken. It is an essential part of personal development to become a better person.

The contact with what you are feeling at each moment is useful not to lose information first hand, because a later analysis, we may not remember all the relevant elements of that experience and those experiences fall within the forgetting curve.

Reflection and daily analysis are essential to locate ourselves in the here and now, to explore ourselves and perceive our most intimate thoughts and feelings.

The opportune moments to do it can be in the night before the hour of sleeping; also, it is adequate during the bath, where relaxed there is the opportunity to contact you and analyze you.

It is advisable to look for the moment and a quiet place where you get the space and time interval long enough to concentrate and contact yourself. It is basic to separate yourself a little from the external stimuli and see inside and imbibe yourself with your senses in what is happening inside of you.

For their part, the Japanese practice Zen where they apply concentration, relaxation, and meditation in a comfortable and peaceful place. They have practiced for more than one thousand 1000 years; obtaining excellent results of physical and psychological health.

This method allows us to concentrate on a point, and through it, to unite with ourselves, feel in tune with our deepest feelings and visualize the brightest of ideas.

A technique used to analyze is through dreams, this allows contact with what happens in the unconscious.

For psychoanalysts, dreams are a window into the depths of our psyche; therefore, the dream is a suitable opportunity to know what is happening in us and what motivates or worries us around us.

There are two relevant aspects in the analysis of our dreams: the first refers to the impression or emotion at the end of the dream; this impression says a lot about the nature of it; and second, the dream can be told to another person or to yourself as if you were living it at that moment, stopping in the details of it and giving them the possible meanings.

Finally, other opportune moments to evaluate yourself can be after a complete physical exercise which allows us to relax and contact with our body and then with our mind and emotions; We must remind ourselves that body and mind is one.

How to Find Me

Lately, do you feel a little lost? Do you feel that the life you lead does not favor you? It is possible that, after carrying obligations for a while, you have lost the "plot" and do not know very well where you are going. When it comes down to this point it is important to stop everything and spend time in meditation, reflection, and calm. Do not forget that your well-being is a priority in your life and, therefore, it is essential that you stop taking the stress and that you focus on yourself. For this reason, we will help you answer your question "How to find me?" so you can recover the spark of your life.

How to Find Yourself and Gain Self-Esteem: The Best Advice

If you want to know how to find yourself, it is important that you stop for a moment and think about yourself. We know that many times, the frenzy of life prevents us from focusing on what is important. We spend more hours working, cooking or sleeping than thinking about whether the life we lead really satisfies us. But if you are reading this book, it is because deep down you know that there is something that does not quite go well. And what can you do to improve it?

The first thing is to stop. Stop devoting so much time and energy to the trivial things in life and start to analyze what is happening to you. If you want to find yourself, it is because you feel that right now, the person who lives in you does not recognize you at all. And it's time to reconnect with your authentic essence and be yourself again.

Here we give you some good tips that will help you to find your way back and recover your authentic "I".

Define Your Goals

This is the first thing you have to do to recover your path and redirect yourself. What do you want from life? Where do you want to go? These are basic questions that you have to start asking so you know what the direction you have to start taking is. Many times, we get lost because we see the future very far or because we focus more on living the present, however, we must never lose sight of what our goal is so to try to get closer to it step by step.

Create Your Own Opinion

It is also possible that right now you do not know exactly who you are because you have not even given yourself time to listen to yourself. What do you think of what is happening around you? In order to find your point of view it is important that you inform yourself, that you look for different points of view and that, after analyzing them, you draw your own conclusions. Dedicating time to critical thinking is essential to be able to define your personality and know who you are.

Dedicate Time to What You Like

In order to find yourself, it is also essential that you do not give up your hobbies or stop doing what really fills you and you like it. We know that routine and obligations can make you leave them in the background and prioritize what you think is "essential." But do not make mistakes: you are the most essential thing there is. So, take care of yourself, pamper yourself, and dedicate time to enjoy life. In the end, that's the only thing you'll get.

Explore Yourself and Know Your "I" Now

But, in addition to the hobbies you've always had, it is likely that, now, you have some new interests that you are not allowing yourself to discover because of the lack of time that haunts us. It is important that we let ourselves evolve and allow ourselves to learn new things to continue growing and enjoying all the opportunities that life gives us. So, allow yourself to sign up for that course or activity that attracts your attention over and over again.

Change What You Do Not Like About Yourself

And, finally, you may feel lost in life because there are some reactions or situations of yourself that you do not like how you manage them. Instead of letting go and turning your back on this problem, it is vital that you face them and that you find some remedy. Is there something about you that you do not like how you solve it? Well, work to change it or improve it. Everything depends on you, so do not forget that you are the owner of your life.

How to Find Myself Again: Techniques for Each Day

In addition to the advice we have given previously that will help you to solve your doubt about "How to find myself?" you have to know that there are other techniques that will help you make this change. You should know that this will not be something that you can change overnight, and for that reason, every day you have to work to find your way. Here we leave some of the most interesting tips that you can apply from now on.

Seek Solitude

Being alone is essential to connect with your interior and know what you want from life. As we have already said, the trick to be able to find oneself is to take an inner journey and analyze the current situation in which one lives. And this work of introspection can only be done in a separate and individual way. So, do not be afraid to be alone and look for it. In this way, you will be able to find you in the middle of the solitude.

Positive Thinking

It is essential that you try to neutralize that little negative voice that you have in your mind and that you start letting the positive one float.

To find your way, it is essential that you are optimistic and you trust yourself, your abilities, and your effort. Only then, will you be able to orientate yourself towards the future you want and, also, have the life that you are interested in having? Do not forget: you can do everything you propose.

Open Up to New People

Many times, getting to know new people gives us the possibility of knowing other ways of living and seeing the world. It is something vibrant and interesting that can serve as inspiration or motivation. Therefore, bring out your most social side and open up to meet new people. You will see how good it is for you!

Leave Your Comfort Zone

Just as it is interesting to meet new people, it is also interesting that you dare to move in new circles. Leaving the comfort zone where you are safe and quiet will show you a part of yourself that, perhaps, you did not know. In addition, this will also allow you to get in touch with other ways of living, other hobbies and other perspectives that you may not even know existed.

Start Meditating

And, finally, another technique that can help you find yourself is to practice meditation. It is a perfect exercise to connect with your interior, calm your mind and concentrate on your emotions and your well-being. It is more than advisable that you begin to meditate when you live a somewhat convulsive or unstable time. It will help you a lot to feel better.

Chapter 3 - Word Clues

What Does A Person Say About Their Speech and The Words They Choose?

Several studies have shown the link between personality and language. For example, an outgoing person and a more sociable person do not talk in the same way.

The Tests

Not all the findings are quite surprising. Those who are very outgoing are noisy and like to talk much more than introverted people. Extrovert women are more likely to have chat groups, while introverted men talk more to themselves. Both make very different use of speech.

A few years ago, a group of researchers did a study on 40 volunteers. In the experiment, they were asked to observe a picture of different social situations and describe out loud what was happening.

The extroverts say: "Let's eat." Introverts say: "Maybe we can go somewhere to eat."

Psychology of The Word

Most of the extroverts enjoy an accelerated life, they like to drink more, to spend the night in any place and to run more risks than the introverts. Every time they open their mouths, extroverts are also ready to face risks with the precision, spontaneity, and scope of what they say. This link between personality and language also extends to the written word.

However, the issue is not limited to extroverts versus introverts. On the contrary, when extroverts talk to each other, they deal with a very diverse range of topics, particularly the "pleasant ones" ("I like to jog," "Soccer is wonderful").

These days' people also spend more time sending emails, writing content for blogs and social networks. And through these routes, we also reveal our personality.

In this sense, those who experience emotional disturbances use these words in a freer way. Extroverts say: "We are so happy." Neurotics say: "I'm having a great time." Incredible as it may seem, this allows us to guess precise psychological traits of their authors.

It Is Inevitable

It seems impossible to avoid trying to decipher the personality of another person because of the language he uses. People continue to judge others even by identity in the digital world.

At the same time, we think that directions made with a sense of humor belong to extroverted people which may not be true. Being aware of how much is revealed is essential. It is somewhat disconcerting, especially for those who like to maintain a profile in private. However, it also offers an opportunity to change the way other people portray you.

In some situations, such as in a job interview or when you start dating, it is possible to adopt a more attractive profile just by changing the language used.

Punctuality

Being unpunctual denotes a certain lack of concern and is not always synonymous with disregard. There are people who cannot avoid it and according to a study, there are four profiles that respond to this attitude, which often mix.

There is a perfectionist, who is late because he cannot leave the house if everything is not in optimum condition. The one that lives to the limit and that always hurries all the circumstances that surround him. To the defiant, the rules do not care, while the dreamer believes that he comes to everything and may not realize his delay.

Nervous Tics

Scientists recorded several individuals in a stressful situation to see how they reacted. And they observed that most perfectionists bit their nails, pulled their hair or pinched themselves during that time. A set of reactions also unfolded in moments of boredom, frustration, and impatience.

The Mobile

The excessive attachment to the mobile can reveal an addiction. Looking at the mobile phone screen constantly is a symptom of emotional instability. A state that can easily lead to addiction to the phone - one of the evils of the times. The study also shows that the shyest and introverted people are the ones who run the least risk of falling into this addiction.

Selfies

The selfies are neither innocent nor spontaneous at times. Self-portraits reveal a world language non-verbal to researchers:

- The friendliest people tend to be photographed from below
- The most scrupulous hardly show the space they are in
- The extroverts and open to new experiences appear in positive attitudes
- Neurotic people tend to put on a duck face

At the Table

Certain behaviors at the table betray certain aspects of the personality. Our personality is expressed at the table, in the way we eat. Those who eat unhurriedly, savoring and chewing each bite conscientiously, are controlling people, sure of themselves and who know how to appreciate life. Those who gobble up without chewing are individuals accustomed to doing a thousand things at once, healthy competitors and with a head that thinks at the speed of light. In relationships, they tend to put the interests of others before their own, while at the same time needing to enjoy their own space.

Some people organize food by color, size or origin. These are people who need order and cleanliness to live quietly. At work, they are organized people, but little resolved in the face of unforeseen and stressful situations.

The controllers, the fussy, the adventurers, the competitors or the planners are manifested at the table.

Adventurers love to try new foods and dishes. They are people who are not bored, risky and extroverted who tend to like everyone.

In this case, it is about individuals who always eat the same food one after another, without mixing. His personality is analytical, detailed, methodical, and can touch the rigidity if it is taken to an extreme.

Nor do those who like to mix food agree with the isolated ones. They are strong, friendly and responsible people, although at work they may lack practicality to know how to prioritize.

Eating quickly indicates nervousness. Those who sip and chew with their mouths open and make noise also denote a personality. In this case, they are carefree people, who do not care what others think of them. Profiles are frank and direct that do not always like everyone.

The planner does not like the unexpected and at the table is the guy who cuts and prepares the food before starting to eat. Accustomed to living in the future, it is difficult to be in the here and now and enjoy. Finally, the fussy person needs to know everything about what he is going to put in his mouth. He grows in his comfort zone and is not used to risk, although this does not prevent him from being curious.

Chapter 4 - Interpreting Behavior Common Patterns and Analysis

Every tragic event makes us think of our own security. We would all like to know what misfortunes and fatalities await us in the future to be able to avoid them in time. But, fortunately, or unfortunately, this knowledge is beyond our reach. However, the years of experience of experts allowed identifying 6 basic characteristics that are inherent to potential criminals. Thanks to these signals, it is not difficult to realize if a person can represent a danger to society.

Change in Self-Perception

The psycho-emotional portrait of most criminals contains a common detail: a pronounced maximalist or minimalism in judgments, including self-perception. A person can exaggerate his own meaning to be considered a representation of the highest or, on the contrary, minimize their role in society.

For example, ore of the attackers wrote in his personal diary: "I am God." This is a clearly expressed radical idea of his superiority over others. Undoubtedly, even without special education, it is possible to notice this type of deviations in human behavior. Especially if they are atypical for the person in question.

How it manifests:

- Manic desire to express racial, gender, social and other types of superiority over others;
- Unconscious underestimation of their importance to the rest of the world, relatives, and friends;
- Categorical refusal to consider any other point of view that differs from their own.

Tendency Towards Dangerous Hobbies

It is worth saying that interest in cold or fire weapons is not a direct sign that a person is a potential criminal. Legal hunting, the collection of rare knives or rifles, the love of computer shooting games is nothing more than a hobby. It is important to see and understand the line that separates a hobby from the manic tendency to deadly dangers.

But if a person admires psychopaths and criminals, expresses approval and respect for some radical ideas and goals, openly expresses extremism, it is a good reason to stay away.

Lack of Empathy for Another Person

As a general rule, a person with a tendency to self-destruction eradicates the feeling of compassion and empathy for others. In general, these people lie very well, are prone to violence and enjoy the torture and humiliation of other people.

The modern world is used to expressing their emotions and preferences in the most simple and accessible way: through social networks. Videos of category 18+ with scenes of cruelty and violence, aggressive appeals and slogans, membership in radical communities, are an important part of what should cause concern. Just looking at the content that interests a person, you can often understand what is more focused.

How it manifests itself:

- Inability to sincere repentance for the works performed

- The person does not express concern for the people around them
- The person does not care about their own physical and emotional health
- Great ability to manipulate other people to achieve their own goals.

Clear Mental Disorders

In this case, we are talking about inappropriate behavior that differs from established norms. It can be obvious aggressiveness or hatred towards other people and animals, mood swings for no reason, attempts to withdraw and abstract. In reality, the symptoms are many, but people who know their problems can hide them well. After all, in criminal practice, there are many cases of violent psychopaths that in the family environment were quite common people.

How it manifests:

- Altered mental activity and behavioral reactions
- Irrational aggression and sudden mood swings

- Behavior that goes beyond the limits of existing moral and cultural norms
- The person may feel inexplicably happy or unhappily unimportant about the events that occurred
- Vague awareness of reality and inadequate perception of one's state

Problems in Contacting the Outside World

The desire to abstain from the outside world can arise for a number of reasons. It can be caused by a prolonged illness, a mental disorder, a long vacation or excessive use of modern technology.

The tendency to de-socialize in adolescents, school children or university students is often caused by bullying: psychological terror, persecution, beatings, and humiliation of one person by another. Children and acolescents, as a rule, try to hide this type of aggressive manifestations from others, considering it shameful. If you notice that your friend, son or relative is under pressure, then in no way should you turn a blind eye.

Depression

Here we are talking about real depression, not stress or a sad spell of bad luck. It is very important to distinguish these concepts, since depression is a mental disorder, while stress or a sad spell of bad luck is quite a natural phenomenon in the life of a person.

The experts distinguish several types of this disease, but all are united by these symptoms:

- Apathy and lethargy, indifference, lack of emotions and desires
- Sleep disorders, anxiety, fear, loss of concentration
- Low self-esteem, a desire to hide from society
- Thoughts about death, suicide, the afterlife, concentration on the negative moments of life
- Alcohol abuse, refusal to eat or tendency to overeat, unwillingness to take care of one's appearance

What Is the Conclusion?

We all sometimes want to be alone, we all have bad mood days and even emotional overflows. So, before drawing conclusions, you must analyze all the components of the person's behavior, because many of our actions depend on the context of the situations in which we find ourselves.

And remember that most tragic events could have been avoided if someone had asked for help from another person on time.

Human Behavior Is Predictable By 93%

A study reveals certain patterns in our mobility, such as the fact that we always return to sites already visited. A team of researchers studied the mobility of thousands of people through the signals of their mobile phones. Thus, they have discovered that our displacements are always highly predictable, regardless of whether we move large or short distances. Knowing the patterns of human mobility, which are maintained in different social groups and environments, could serve to optimize urban development and public health policies.

What We Think About Our Future Determines Our Happiness

The electrical activity of the heart can already be simulated. Study shows that body language expresses our socioeconomic status. Religion is an effective regulator of human behavior. Some human behaviors have an evolutionary background. Human behavior is predictable by 93%, says a group of scientists.

The researcher came to this conclusion from an investigation in which the displacement patterns of anonymous users of mobile telephony were studied.

Specifically, the journeys of a total of 50,000 people, chosen at random from a set of 10 million individuals, were analyzed over three months. This study has revealed that, although it is generally believed that most of the actions that we take are unpredictable and random however humans follow regular patterns most of the time.

Spontaneous People Are Scarce

Spontaneous individuals are scarce among the population. Thus, although significant differences have been found in the travel patterns among the individuals studied, the movements of each one of them, separately, are equally predictable.

This predictability is, as has been said, of 93%, regardless of the distance that people travel when traveling: whether they move far from their homes or stay close to them, you can "guess" with the same exactitude they will find out in the next hour.

Another researcher points out that people usually assume that it is easier to predict people that travel very less as compared to people that travel over a thousand kilometers.

Back to The Known

However, this study has shown that, despite the heterogeneity of displacements, the movement of all individuals falls within what is expected.

Research has also shown another surprising aspect of population mobility: patterns of individual movements do not vary significantly depending on certain demographic categories, such as age, sex, population density or whether the location studied is rural or urban

In other previous research on mobility patterns, researchers studied the trajectories in real time of 100,000 anonymous mobile phone users. These users were also selected randomly, from a list of more than six million people.

In this case, the results were similar to those of the present investigation: the scientists verified that, in spite of the diversity of the travel history of each of the individuals analyzed, all followed reproducible mobility patterns.

For example, people, for more or fewer kilometers that travel, always have a strong tendency to return to locations they have visited previously.

What It Is For

As the scientists published, foreseeing the movements of people could serve as a management resource for mobile communications.

On the other hand, it would also be useful to make models for the expansion of epidemics, to carry out better urban planning or to design traffic more efficiently.

In general, being able to know scientifically how the population is going to move could have a positive impact on society, on public health policies and on urban development.

Be A Model of Behavior for A Teenager

When we talk about influencing behavior, one of the most powerful tools is role modeling. Finding an appropriate model of behavior for a teenager or being ourselves is one of the most effective methods to get him to change his habits.

In this section, we will talk about the importance of modeling and how to get your child to change through the imitation of other people or yourself. Keep in mind that modeling is one of the tools you can use to change your child's behavior.

Psychology has traditionally studied imitation. Human beings are social beings and nature has endowed us with an innate capacity to learn from others by repeating their behavior.

This is a fabulous way to maintain the culture at the level of society, but it is also a way to achieve a specific change in behavior in those who need it.

The basic idea of this technique is simple. Your child can change his behavior by watching other people do it and evaluating the consequences for them.

Imagine possible scenarios:

Discover the best educational tools to connect with your adolescent child. A course specially designed to improve communication at home and the motivation of your child.

Learn or increase a behavior before a model that gets rewards: think of a small child who sees another child get what he wants from adults when he cries or howls.

I remember the story of a friend who at 3 years old recognized being the class bully. He had a voice so unusually powerful for his age that when he cried, he frightened the rest of his classmates. Only for the teacher to shut up gave her any whim she had. Today, my friend admits having used this ability to make a profit. Sadly, other children of that same class learned their tricks from him, distributing not a few headaches among their families. In this example, the key is that my friend was publicly rewarded for his screams.

Decrease or eliminate a behavior in front of a punished model. As intelligent animals, we run away from situations in which we see others get into trouble. Imagine that your child contemplates how his classmates laugh at a boy with glasses. It is very likely that if one day he needs them he will resist using them or will ask you to wear contact lenses to avoid being discriminated against.

In both examples, there is a model that obtains some consequences of its social group for its behaviors. The people who surround this model learn from these consequences and try to repeat or avoid their behavior depending on whether they are rewarded or punished.

Characteristics of An Effective Model

As human beings, we have the ability to imitate models from our birth. This ability has been related to cooperative skills, socialization, and empathy.

Our brain contains a series of mirror neurons that are closely related to this ability. Thanks to them we can learn from the behaviors of other people just by observing them.

Interestingly, this ability to learn through imitation and mirror neurons has also been found in other animals such as primates and some birds. Therefore, it is not an exclusively human capacity.

Research on the type of behavior model for an adolescent has found some common characteristics:

They imitate people that are considered competent and are prestigious or have a social status.

Those people similar in age, sex and ethnicity will be considered as a model to imitate with greater probability. At this point, children and adolescents are an exception since they tend to imitate adult models as well.

They tend to emulate those models that obtain positive consequences for their observed behaviors. My friend was imitated by his companions because shouting invariably won a prize.

Television as A Role Model for A Teenager

One of the curiosities that have been found in research on imitation is that modeling can occur from a person present or be symbolic, without there being a real reference.

That is to say, learning and imitating behavior can be produced by watching a video or listening to a sound recording. This is a very common phenomenon that happens continuously in our society, also in the adult world.

We can even affirm that television is the main behavioral model of our society. Films and advertising are two great schools of conduct for us and day by day they create a trend in our culture.

Television can become a role model for a teenager. Just think about how the European Union faced the power of the big tobacco companies to ban tobacco advertising in the press, radio, and Internet starting in 2005.

Parents in the Cloud Courses

Sign up for the best courses to educate your adolescent child. You will discover the most effective techniques to achieve an improvement in communication and motivation in your home.

It is difficult to know which models your child will choose to imitate during his adolescence. But you can try to become a model. For this, we propose the following strategies that as a parent you can use to achieve it.

Use more than one model whenever possible: studies show that it is much more effective if the behavior occurs in several people. Imagine that you educate your son so that he does not smoke and you are a model for him because you do not do it. Imitation will be much more effective if neither your partner nor your school teachers smoke. This is effective because it will make more credible for your child what you observe. That is, the greater the number of models that comply with the behavior, the greater the probability of imitation.

Pose behaviors to imitate that do not exceed the capacity of your child: it seems obvious but think if sometimes you have expected your child to imitate your behaviors that he may not understand or may not be able to repeat. Ideally, the behavior model for an adolescent of this type of complex behavior begins with simple acts and gradually becomes more complicated. A typical example of this point would be that your child is able to make the purchase independently. Although now you do not see it, this behavior includes many repertoires of different abilities that you can divide and go modeling little by little. Locate the products, calculate the price, interact with the supermarket workers and so on.

Perception of the consequences of the behaviors: it will be much more effective for your child to see how a friend of his who has disrespected a teacher gets his punishment. If this happens, you can anticipate the consequences of repeating those types of behaviors and it will be easier for you not to repeat them.

Reward the successes: if your son manages to replicate the behavior you want him to imitate, reward him for it. It will be the best way to accelerate the imitation process and thus you will understand directly that you are on the right track and that you have your approval.

Chapter 5 - Speed reading

Speed reading is a technique to increase reading without compromising understanding and retention of information. There are several different methods of speed reading, but they all aim to read clearly, but faster.

For those who work as a freelancer, especially the producers of web content, digital marketing, etc., reading is a prime activity. And speed reading lets you take even more of the time you have available for this activity. It is through reading that you deepen your knowledge to argue more strongly and keep your repertoire of subjects relevant and up to date.

Unfortunately, it is not always possible to devote the time needed to complete reading an article or a book. In this situation, speed reading helps you extract the most important information in less time.

What Is Speed Reading?

Speed reading is a technique that seeks to increase the reading speed without compromising understanding and retention of information.

There are several different speed-reading methods for both books and online texts and they all aim to read clearly as well as faster.

Check out this step by step guide and learn how to enhance your speed-reading skills!

1. Train your eyes to make bigger jumps

Do you know how the movement of your eyes works while reading? Basically, it's a jumping move. Your eyes pin one point on the line and then jump to the next.

The higher this leap, the more proficient is your reading. Beginner readers, like children, skip only one word at a time and therefore take longer to finish each line. Therefore, the first step of speed reading is to train the eye movement so that it is wider.

2. Go straight ahead

The second step is to control that anxiety, that sense of obligation to understand 100% of the text. We are going to take this up further, but know that 80% understanding is an excellent goal.

In other words, you do not have to return to the beginning of the page every time you co not understand a line. After all, re-reading can take a long time - anc that is precisely what we are trying to avoid.

In addition, you can fully understand the general idea of a text, even though some excerpts are more confusing. Then, after finishing the text, resume only the parts where you have doubts. But if you stop and go back constantly, you will never finish reading.

Another important tip is to not interrupt the reading to check the dictionary. If you are very curious about the meaning of a word, write it down to check later. However, do not abandon the text to browse the dictionary because when you return, it will take you even longer to resume reading.

In the meantime, try to understand the term by context - you may not absorb the exact meaning of the word, but it will be enough to understand the message the author wanted to convey.

3. Stop speaking the words

The third step is to eliminate a negative practice that is a habit of many people: to pronounce the words as they read, either loudly or mentally.

This habit prevents the development of speed reading because it means that you will literally read word for word.

The speed slows down and as incredible as it may seem, the capacity for understanding as well. Because your brain will be busy with pronunciation, you will not be able to concentrate on interpreting what you are reading. The result is that you will have to reread the same stretch several times.

If you are too accustomed to pronounce as you read, losing this habit can be a difficult and time-consuming process. An interesting tip is to put a pencil in your mouth as you read. With a little practice, you will lose this "craze" and see how it improves your reading time.

4. Use skimming technique

The fourth step is "skimming." This is a well-known technique for Instrumental English, but it is also useful for speed reading in any language.

Skimming consists basically of looking quickly through a text in order to extract basic information - index, title, author, date of publication, main subject, subtopics developed, graphics and images.

This technique is useful for you to quickly evaluate any text and then set whether to devote more time to a full reading.

If you are researching on a specific subject, for example, skimming will allow you to identify whether a particular article or book has relevant information about the subject. In addition, you will find the excerpts that interest you more easily.

5. Use the scanning technique

The fifth step, "scanning," is another technique used in English Instrumental. It consists basically of looking at the text to identify keywords, which in this case are relevant terms, related to the information you want to extract from that content.

Suppose you are reading a twenty-page article on People Management, but the subject that really matters to you is Productivity. In that case, you do not have to read all twenty pages - which will certainly tell you about various other issues that are not important to you right now.

Instead, just look through the article for terms directly related to productivity, such as "time," "organization," "concentration," and so on. When you find one of these terms, you just need to read that passage. Thus, you quickly get information that is of interest to you and "skip" the rest.

6. Monitor your performance

Once you incorporate what you have learned in the first five steps, the evolution of your speed reading will depend on practice. But to see if it's working, you need to keep track of your progress.

So, the sixth step is picking up a timer and monitoring how many words you read per minute. As a reference, keep in mind that a typical reader reads, on average, 150 words per minute. Meanwhile, a good speed-reading practitioner can read up to 800 words per minute.

But do not just monitor speed. Take into account, also, the use of reading, that is, how much you can understand the text without having to return to it a second time. Your goal should be an average of 80% utilization.

Remember that there is no point in speeding up reading, and thereby lessening the understanding of what has been read, as the re-reading also represents a waste of time.

7. Train Your Focusing Ability

Now that we've covered the best strategies for speed reading itself, let's take a few tips that will enhance your reading experience as a whole and as a result, help you absorb more information in less time.

The ability to stay focused while reading is critical to being productive and not wasting time. The deeper you "plunge" into the text, the better you understand what the author wrote.

What happens, then, if you go to every two paragraphs to check the notifications on your cell phone? The experience will be interrupted and continually resumed, which diminishes your ability to comprehend and thus takes you to take more time to understand what is read.

In this way, you waste twice as much time: the extra time it takes to understand what you read and the precious minutes wasted with distractions (Smartphone, computer, social networks, etc.).

If you often suffer from it, the key is to turn productivity into a habit. To do so, when you read, keep the distractions away. This means not leaving the phone nearby, not keeping the computer by your side and, if possible, turning off the internet or at least placing your devices in airplane mode.

This time is for you to dedicate to the text and nothing else! The more you can focus on reading, the better your ability to practice speed reading.

8. Find a quiet place to do your reading

The place you choose to do your readings also greatly influences the speed and dynamism of the activity - something very connected to the danger represented by the distractions, as we just mentioned.

Noise from traffic, from work, from an establishment (such as a bar, for example) and even from music can disturb your ability to concentrate, making you frequently "quit" reading. Also, if you are reading in an environment with other people, you will also be directly interrupted if they speak to you, even if it is a quick dialogue.

Besides being silent, it is also important that the chosen corner for reading is comfortable. When you are comfortable reading, it is much easier to indulge in the text and devote your full attention to it. And if you have a special space where you like to read, another advantage is that this will make it easier to establish reading as an integral part of your routine.

9. Do not insist when you are tired

You may have heard that it is not very productive for a student to spend the night studying for a test that will be given the next day. At that point, the desperation of a few extra hours of study is no longer as important as the rest, which will allow more focus and better memory for the student during the test.

The same principle can be applied to speed reading. When we are tired, regardless of whether the exhaustion reaches our site and/or head, our ability to concentrate decreases dramatically. You will find yourself having to read and reread the same passage several times, and of course, it takes much longer to read each line.

And the worst part is that the next day you can pick up the text and realize you cannot remember much of anything you read the night before. This is because a tired brain also decreases its ability to retain information.

So, an important point of speed reading is to know the time to stop.

10. Read whenever you can

What the reader does not like to sit in their favorite armchair and deliver hours and hours to a book or even a relevant and high-quality text? However, as you well know, this is not always (or rather, almost never!) possible.

Does this mean, then, that you are bound to a routine? Of course not! It turns out you do not have to self-punch yourself for not being able to devote several hours of each day to reading.

Start enjoying every free minute, especially with regards to idle time spent in queues, waiting rooms, or on public transportation, for example. And how about going a little early to bed, every night, and reading before bed?

A block of fifteen or twenty minutes in which you would do nothing when dedicated to reading becomes time well spent. With this, you advance much faster in your readings, although you cannot read much each day. Anotl er advantage is that this will help you build the daily habit of reading - and, who knows, it will even encourage you to separate a few hours of your day into the activity.

Do you already practice speed reading? What is your speed and reading achievement? If you have not yet reached the goals proposed here, do not wcrry. Reading is a habit you cannot be afraid to develop, and the benefits are gigantic.

Keep in mind, however, that the tendency is to improve your vocabulary with constant reading. And with a complete vocabulary, you will have more and more facility to read and understand longer texts.

Essential Tips You Should Know About Speed Reading

Learn how to read more quickly by ensuring that all the content you learn is not lost in your mind after a few days.

Answer quickly! Do you read fast or slow? Have you ever tried to calculate your reading speed? By chance, have you heard of dynamic reading?

If not, you should. Well, if you love reading or even depending on it for studies, this advanced reading mode could help you a lot!

Dynamic reading is a faster type of reading which makes you read a lot in a short time. You may be thinking: reading fast is easy, but you cannot memorize it that way. Therefore, dynamic reading ensures this without impairing its ability to absorb content.

We've prepared some essential tips for you to start increasing your reading speed.

Understand: There are different types of reading speed. There are some reading differences that you may not know about and it is important to know. As we said, a more agile and concentrated reading reduces the time needed for learning. Therefore, it optimizes productivity and ensures that all content learned is not lost in your mind after a few days.

And this is essential for students, contestants, or even law and medical market professionals who need to read constantly. But this is not restricted to a group of people. Dynamic reading can help someone who already has a habit of reading to make you a reader with an even greater repertoire.

It must be understood that dynamic reading has two fundamental factors: content speed and retention. In short, reading too slowly can hinder the progress of any reading, or studies. Just like reading too fast and not understanding the subject is not good either.

Therefore, it is essential to find a balance by reading at a fast speed that does not detract from the retention of information.

Valuable tips for anyone who wants to start dynamic reading!

- Start slowly. Read every 15 minutes free!
- Subtract only minutes from your daily activities to read.
- Walk around with a book in hand and use short spaces of time to read.
- Read for 20 minutes while waiting for dinner to be ready in the oven.

- Read while waiting for the bus to work and if possible, even within driving.

With time and practice, dynamic reading will already be in your effortlessly!

Take A Test to Know How Long Your Reading Speed Is!

The measure used to calculate the reading speed is the number of words read per minute (PPM). Usually, an average person with a reading habit reads about 250 words per minute. To know how to calculate, follow these steps:

Count the number of words in the first 3 lines of the same text. If you are reading in Word, it shows you how many words in the text.

Divide the total number of words from the first 3 lines by 3. The result will be the average number of words per line.

Multiply the average number of words per line by the number of lines you read in a minute. The end result will be your PPM index.

Let's see in practice:

Let's say that the first three lines of a text have 29 words. Therefore, the average number of words per line would be 9.6 (29/3 = 9.6). Now imagine that you have read 30 lines of that same text in 1 minute. In this case, its result would be 288 PPM (30 × 9.6).

That is, a result of an ordinary reader, but still slightly above the average of 250 PPM.

Now that you have the result in hand, start with the first tip. Start by reading slowly for a few minutes. When you feel comfortable, improve your reading speed. Therefore, determine a goal for yourself and try to fulfill it. You must have a goal before anything else.

Redo the calculations. Do not worry if you initially get below average. It is totally understandable and normal. In fact, if you are well above average, you probably have not performed the exercise correctly. And there is only one way of knowing if you have unconsciously not sabotaged yourself: try to explain the content of what has been read to someone. This is the best way to prove that your content retention was good.

Increase your reading speed. The best way to read faster is to practice reading every day. The more you read, the faster it gets. And you can start doing that already.

Chapter 6 - Cold Reading

Cold Reading has been used for years by so-called "seers," "gurus," "mentalists," "hypnotists," to impress people and quickly create a connection with another person.

Why Use Cold Reading?

More recent studies on Cold Reading have built conclusions more favorable than unfavorable. An important point to note is that when you do a "negative" reading of a person, it is usually difficult to get a positive reaction from it. This reflects when we read something positive or good about a person. This is because people usually see themselves as good people more than others. However, just to conclude, the most incredible effect I can fit into Cold Reading is the ability to convey to others the kindness that is sometimes hidden or erased, but which is certainly present in each of us.

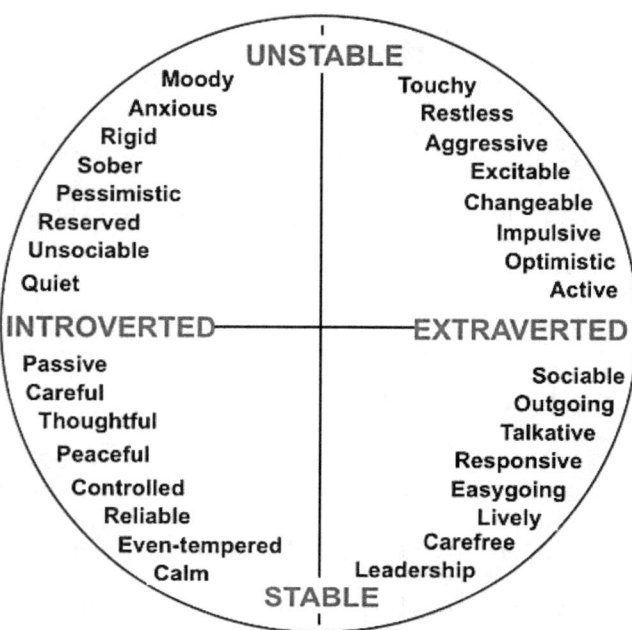

With Cold Read it is possible to elicit reflective states about certain beliefs that the person possesses, for example:

"You have much strength and strength to fight for the dreams and goals you want to achieve, but never forget to help the people you love."

"You're a reserved person and you hardly show what you're feeling, but when you show that you like attention and respect."

"You are a person who understands the difficulties of others, likes to know how the people you love the most and even get involved psychologically in matters that neither would need"

In addition to eliciting beliefs, check out the Cold Read utility roll below.

- Making friends
- Seducing the opposite sex
- Making people reveal something that is secret
- Starting a conversation
- Helping people open up and venting
- Making deep subtle compliments
- Picking up the car esteem of someone
- Create a genuine connection
- Insert thoughts
- Enable emotional triggers
- Intimidate
- Impress
- Searching the truth

Of course, for you to achieve the above goals would be great if you had sentences ready so that you can choose which ones to use as needed.

Cold Reading: Definition, Techniques, and Examples

Much of the Cold Read effect was created to impress. When we pretend to know more than a certain person thought we knew, here comes an immediate effect, as if it were a mental pattern of astonishment that is activated. From there, you can be seen as a leader, guru, seer and etc.

Of course, in addition, by Cold Reading, you can reach times when the person is going to vent with the reader. Sometimes when a reader encounters a serious subject such as poorly resolved personal problems, anxiety problems, the ethical reader slows down reading and becomes a good listener. After that, the reader helps this troubled person find professional help. This may be the highest act of Cold Read ethics, a counselor in crisis, a shelter, or even the police in case of dangerous or abusive people in the relationship.

These actions will lead you to be a person who seeks to help people, unlike those who only seek to personally benefit from the unhappiness of others.

Ethical cold readers always use their abilities to have an influence on the lives of the people who play it. Here are some guidelines to follow:

- Never say you have supernatural abilities;
- Never use Cold Reading in a context of religion;
- Never intend to communicate with deceased persons;
- Never fraudulently induce a subject to have additional readings;

Even when a reader relieves himself of having paranormal abilities, the effect of Cold Reading is so powerful that some viewers begin to claim that the reader has paranormal powers. In this case, what remains is to understand this fact and explore the immoral reasons for not propagating such absurdity.

Chapter 7 - Analyzing Personality Types

Researchers examined data that was collected from over 1.5 million people and it was found that there is a minimum of four distinct personality groups: reserved, regular, exemplary, and egocentric. The findings go against the existing paradigms that are present in psychology.

The study used questionnaires with questions, in which volunteers volunteered to respond in exchange for more information about their own personality.

People have tried to sort out personality types since ancient times, but the scientific literature has discovered that this did not make sense.

Personality types were only found in self-help literature and did not find any mention in scientific journals. From the answers of the questionnaires, the specialists pointed out the five basic traits of personality: neuroticism, extraversion, openness to new experiences, sympathy, and conscientiousness. Once the new algorithms were developed, there were four types of personalities that emerged.

Regular

Regular people are rich in neuroticism and extraversion, and have low levels of openness to new experiences. Women are usually more prone to fall into this category.

Reserved

The reserved individual is emotionally stable but has no openness or neuroticism. He is not extroverted, but he is pleasant and aware.

Exemplary

Exemplary people score low on neuroticism and high on all other characteristics. There are more women in this category. The likelihood of someone being exemplary increases with age. They are the kind of people that you can trust and they are open to new ideas. These are the kind of people that will take care of things.

Egocentric

This group scores very extroversion and below the required score in openness, sympathy, and awareness. These are people you do not want to leave. There has been a substantial decrease in self-centered numbers as peoples age, both with women and men.

Researchers also developed a new method, reducing the possibility of aggregation of the algorithms. This procedure revealed the four groups.

To make sure the categories were accurate, they used a group of egocentrics - adolescent boys - to validate the information. We know that adolescents behave in an egocentric way. "If the algorithms were correct and selected for demographic data, the results would point to the egocentric as the largest group of people in that situation."

According to experts, this research can help health care professionals evaluate people with extreme personalities. In addition, you can collaborate with the selection of candidates in job vacancies or even for those who are looking for a loving partner.

The analysis also points out that as mature people, their personality types changed. For example, older people are usually a lot more conscientious and sympathetic than the people that fall under the age of 20 years. When we look at people in large groups, it becomes very clear that trends exist. Some people can change their characteristics over time.

Classification of Personality Types

The classification of your personality type is by the combination of 4 criteria.

These criteria are the opposite and exclusive. For example, if you are extroverted, you cannot be introverted. In order for a personality to be formed, it is necessary to choose a criterion of each criterion. In the end, the combination of the four chosen criteria gives the personality type, for example, ENTP or INFJ.

Check out the acronyms and the four classification criteria below:

Personality Types: Introverts or Extroverts

The first classification of personality types is related to the way we interact with the world. With respect to this question we can be: Extroverts (E) or Introverts (I):

Extroverts (E): Who has this type of personality is extremely sociable and likes to talk and interact with other people. He is not afraid to state his opinions and is very communicative. Focus your energy on the real world.

Introverts (I): These are usually people who feel better alone, are less sociable, and interact with fewer people. In general, they do not open easily. They concentrate their energy on the world of thoughts.

Types of Personality: Sensory or Intuitive

The second classification of personality types is related to how we observe and absorb information from the world. With respect to this criterion we can be: Sensorial (S) or Intuitive (N):

Sensory (S): Corresponds to the most materialistic personality type, obtains information through the observation of facts and concrete details. They are realistic and practical people.

Intuitive (N): These are people who have a more imaginative profile. Instead of obtaining information through concrete facts, they prefer to observe and draw the final conclusions from their own thoughts and beliefs. They are the most creative and complex people.

Types of Personality: Thinkers or Sentimental

The third classification of personality types concerns how we judge other people's actions and also how we make decisions. With regard to this criterion we can be: Thinkers (T) or Sentimental (F):

Thinkers (T): They make decisions and always judge people based on logic, generally weighing the pros and cons of the situation. They are objective and fair, they rarely let feelings influence their decisions. They value logic, justice, and equality among people.

Sentimental (F): People with this type of personality judge people and make their decisions guided by their instincts and also by feelings (decide based on what they are feeling at the moment). They value harmony, empathy does not follow strict rules, they accept exceptions well.

Types of Personality: Judges or Perceptive

The fourth classification of personality types is related to how we prefer to live, whether we prefer to act spontaneously or whether we prefer to think well before acting. With respect to this criterion we can be: Judges (J) or Perceptive (P):

Judges (J): Whoever has the type of judging personality is satisfied after decisions have been made, they are distressed by letting problems accumulate. In general, do not think much before acting, prefer to regret later.

Perceptive (P): They are more satisfied to make well-thought-out and more accurate decisions; they take time to act. Perceptions become distressed if they need to make a decision quickly. They usually think hard before they act because they are afraid to repent.

Chapter 8 - Verbal & Nonverbal Communication

When we review the parts of the oratory we usually focus on the non-verbal forms, taking for a fact that verbal communication is generated spontaneously and that you can hardly influence it. However, the verbal part of the speech is fundamental, and therefore we must work to make our arguments convincing.

We will analyze what is verbal communication, what is its influence on discourse and how we can improve our verbal expression.

What Is Verbal Communication?

Verbal communication is based on an interaction model in which signs are used to elaborate a message. This definition may sound technical, but it simply refers to the letters, syllables, and words understood as signs, and to their different unions to elaborate complete messages, that other people are capable of understanding and interpreting.

When we talk about oral communication, we usually think of a person who articulates a speech. However, there are two forms of verbal communication:

Oral communication: Includes words verbalized by means of voice and words spoken in a gestural way. For example, in sign language.

Written communication: It is done through written messages that the receiver must read and interpret.

Oral communication is framed in a specific situation that will be decisive for the effectiveness of the message. All these elements must be taken into account in order to construct appropriate messages in form and content.

Issuer: This is the person who generates the message.

Recipient: Is the person who receives the message and interprets it.

Message: The content, the information that goes from the sender to the receiver.

Code: System that we use to articulate the message, usually we identify it with the language.

Channel: Medium through which the message is transmitted.

Context: General situation in which verbal communication is framed. This simple scheme is what will determine the effectiveness of our communication.

The Importance of Verbal Communication in Work Groups

In any methodology that includes working groups, communication is fundamental. Verbal communication is immediate. That's why we use it continuously both to organize groups internally and to exchange messages between different workgroups.

The dynamism and effectiveness of the groups depend on communication. A Scrum process, for example, would be unfeasible without a shared model of communication, and its development is very difficult if verbal communication is deficient.

As we say, communicative analysis tends to focus on most occasions on non-verbal communication. However, functional communication, the one we use continuously and the one that carries the information load is verbal, and therefore we must master it.

Improve Verbal Communication in Our Day to Day

Actually, verbal communication requires a long process of improvement, but we will highlight some aspects that we can improve simply by being aware of our daily verbal messages.

Avoid snitches and phrases. These are very common when you start sentences and they occur unconsciously.

Modulate the tone of your voice. The volume of your message will be based on the message and the environment in which you find yourself.

Pauses and active listening should be part of all your verbal interactions. So important as to what is expressed and what is not said.

Communicate naturally, sometimes adopting certain tones or attitudes makes the defects of oral communication more evident.

You must be clear and precise at all times, regardless of who the recipient is. Two personal traits should accompany our messages: passion (natural y) and education.

Use if possible, the name of your interlocutor, this creates confidence. These are some tips that you can use whether you have to prepare a speech or your day-to-day work environment.

Now we know the importance of speech and oratory, so we prepare specific courses focused on this subject if you want more information contact us.

It is through the study of body language and non-verbal intelligence that we can read and interpret clues.

What Can We Understand By "Non-Verbal Intelligence"?

Non-verbal intelligence focuses on the study of non-verbal communication, analyzing facial expressions, gestures, tone of voice, speed, volume, set of movements and postures, deciphering them as accurately as possible, through context to decode the possible meanings of each of these nonverbal signals.

The body reflects the thoughts and translates into gestures, postures and facial expressions the true feelings of the people. It also reveals their true personality, intentions, degrees of attachment, emotions, interests and even the position they occupy in a conversation.

Not wanting to see or not give importance to these body signals is to lose a large part of the trust and the most secret message of people. Did you know that we emit signs even when we think we do not and do not even notice that we adopt behaviors that denounce us in an obvious way? Too tight a handshake, an intimidating look, scratching your eyebrow when she shows you the new dress, or raising a shoulder when she questions a seller about a product she wants to buy, all of these signs can give clear information about people's intentions.

In fact, it is through the study of body language and non-verbal intelligence that we can read and interpret clues such as gestures, movements, postures or facial expressions that people consciously or unconsciously let go of, which will also protect us from fewer threats or intentions and will still be able to deliver messages in a more effective, engaging, credible way as clearly as possible.

The thought that has always been with me is the idea of reading other people's thoughts, having this power and during the last decades, I tried to get closer to this reading of thoughts and decided to learn everything about how to decipher people with the world's greatest experts, from body language specialists and non-verbal intelligence to former FBI agents, spies, therapists, psychologists, human behavior researchers. I have always had a healthy dose of skepticism coupled with an open mind when exposed to the science's teachings of deciphering people.

The more I learned how to decipher people, the more I was sure that everyday life was getting faster and more fulfilling. It is a general tendency for people to lose interest in detail and pay close attention to what is new. It began to seem strange to me to realize that most people had an almost blind trust in words and the power of perception, ind fferent to nonverbal signals.

I wondered why many people had forgotten the oldest and truest language of the human being. I knew that to master and control this silent language, the art of deciphering people would give me the power to know more about people, about their motivations, their fears, their intentions, and their deepest secrets. By reading the non-verbal signals I was now able to find out more about others and even more about myself. I was able to anticipate behaviors, change communication strategies according to context and protect myself from toxic relationships in order to improve the results of my day -a day.

How is Will Being Unconscious of This Kind of Communication Cause Us to Have the Wrong Perception About Someone?

We can fake body language, but we cannot always pretend. Studies carried out over the years tells us the message between two people face to face is transmitted in the following proportion: 7% verbal communication, 38% refers to the tone of speed (rhythm and volume), and 55% refers to body language, making facial expressions, gestures, tone of voice, speed, rhythm, volume and movement responsibility in the transmission of a message, much more than words.

Both studies reveal the importance of the non-verbal part in the transmission of the message, and many people are aware of these studies, but few remember to apply it because they continue to care more about the words, they are going to say than about how properly they will say them. We are all born to know how to identify facial expressions, gestures, and postures subconsciously and we are also constantly learning new expressions, gestures and their meanings, as a way to protect ourselves during life. It is therefore so important for our protection and success.

Can We Then Conclude That There Are Gestures That Demonstrate Mastery and Others That Demonstrate Submission?

To dominate is the manifestation "fight response" of the limbic system. Even if we are rarely in situations that require real fighting, using our domain is like using our bodies to demonstrate leadership, trust, professionalism, credibility, intimidation, and even when we want to be perceived as more interesting and competent. Mastering prevents you from perceiving us as easy-to-manipulate or easy-to-control "targets", protect us from "predators" (bad bosses, bad salesmen, bad friends ...).

Submission is exactly the opposite of domain, shows the absence of the "fight response". A submissive person may decide that in order to survive, it is best not to generate a fight by agreeing to the dominance exercised so as not to irritate the person who claimed to be dominant.

Have You Ever Wondered Why the Bosses Are the Ones with The Bigger Offices?

One of the manifestations of the dominant is to demand more space. This is a form of territoriality, requiring more space is a territorial issue. Another way to demonstrate this is to move away from the feet, the further away, the greater the demonstration of mastery. The submissive, not to challenge the dominant, occupy less space, joining their feet.

Many of the submissive believe that not confronting the dominant is the best way to please, what happens is that we like people like us and that submission has the opposite effect. To please the dominant, we must also exhibit domain behaviors. We should only emit some submissive behavior in a conscious way and say only a few, in situations where you may be being evaluated or need something from the other person (job interviews, sales, talking to your boss).

What Kind of Nonverbal Signals Exist That Allow You To "Decipher People"?

Deciphering people through body language shares a learning process similar to learning ABC's in school: we will have to learn the simplest and most important signs first and their possible meanings, and then we can begin to put them together so that we can read more people's intentions or thoughts. Let us remember that a gesture, movement or facial expression can have several meanings and depends on the context in which it takes place.

Thus, we can divide the non-verbal signals into five categories, beginning with the "symbols," characterized as movements used instead of words with easily perceived meaning (for example, saying OK by raising the thumb up), and by "illustrators," or movements that accompany speech to illustrate what is being said (for example, counting to four and showing the four fingers).

In addition to these, we also have "regulators," which are defined as movements related to the function of speech and hearing and which indicate intentions (eg, nodding, looking more intensely, changing posture), gestures that regulate the interaction, movements made by the speaker or by whom he listens for the purpose of showing attention, interest or dominion.

Finally, "pacifiers", defined as movements that serve to calm down in situations of discomfort or nervousness (for example, drumming with fingers, pulling hair, playing with a ring) and "indicators", which are movements similar to the illustrators, in the sense that they also accompany words, but differ in one respect: they reflect the emotional state in which the person is at the moment (eg, comfort, discomfort, anxiety, fear, flight).

Which Areas of The Body Show the Most Honest Signs?

To decipher a person, it is not necessary to see more but to see better. It is to be attentive to the signs and to understand the possible meanings and which trigger triggered this same signal. When I started learning how to decipher people, I realized that it was a huge task, I had to simplify and create a system that was effective, because if it works with me, it also works with others, and so I created the system

All the signs I learned fit into these categories. For example, I watched the tension in my lips and wondered what the meaning might be and what category it could fit into. And I would respond to myself: if the tension in the lips is stress or emotional tension, then the person is uncomfortable. Another example is that the person lifts his chin while talking to me: if you lift your chin it is a sign that you do not see me as a threat or with high ego, then you are a dominant one.

The legs, feet, arms, hands, and fingers are responsible for executing the stimuli of the brain: from paralyzing, escaping and struggling to the most primitive instincts in response to the interpretation of external events. It also has as its responsibility for the territorial demonstrations of dominance and the removal of possible threats or "competitors". I see the members as the front line, that is, the protection, connection, struggle or conquest of our deepest feelings, thoughts, and desires.

The legs and feet are the parts of the body that emit the most honest signals of our body, given the greater distance of the brain. We consciously control words, facial expressions, arms, and hands more properly than legs and feet. When I refer to the clues of interest, mastery, or tension, I believe in the messages given by the feet rather than the words because they are easier to manipulate.

Is Not One Running the Risk of Misinterpreting One's Intentions by Seeking Constant Meaning in One's Gestures?

This happens whether or not knowing how to read body language, it is a human need. I want to warn of the tendency we have to imagine meanings, often based on pre-judgments. Whether or not you like a person, this cannot interfere with the reading of your body language; therefore, it is fundamental, to learn the meanings and to be aware of all the stereotypes, in order to avoid prejudices before starting to read body language.

I prefer to believe that it is the result of education, of experiences and of what they have told you that it would be right or wrong from childhood. Sometimes prejudices work in our favor, others may work against us. We should not make pre-judgments based on past experiences and beliefs. It is always less likely to err when we know the meanings of what we are observing.

Is Non-Verbal Communication Always Genuine or Can It Be "Falsified"?

We can disguise, but we cannot hide! There will always be signs that identify our true intent or emotion, these signs being more visible to trained eyes. Body language is responsible for defining how the interactions between two or more people will take place, and not being perceived as confident, credible or honest will greatly hamper their image as we associate nonverbal behaviors with the mentioned characteristics.

There are days or heights of life that we are less well emotionally and the body reveals these same feelings, however many times we are not evaluated by our skills or intentions, but by the perception that people are of our skills or intentions for this reason I recommend study, apply, and master body language to help people gain a more accurate understanding of their essence in different situations or contexts, and this perception will determine the degree of influence they exert and their decision-making power.

Now, more importantly, body language is like clothing, not everything suits us and many people have the perception that just use some postures and gestures to get the right message, however, if the postures used are not according at our core, communication fails. Knowing and applying Body Language techniques is like using a knife, it can be used to do good or bad.

Chapter 9 - Spot Lies, Insecurity and Interests

Ways to Expose A Lie

One person usually tells three lies every ten minutes. This is what the study says. Research indicates that recourse to untruths is a matter of habit and a way of maintaining a good social living.

Types of Lies

People in loving relationships lie more when there are concern and distrust in excess on the part of the other. For them, insecurity creates discomfort and difficulty in revealing the truth. The work also points out that flirtations and attraction for other people, contacts and friendships, level of commitment, sexual fantasies, betrayal, sexual satisfaction, and appearance are also subjecting that the couples usually hide from the partner. Already in the workplace, the expert points out that the most common lies are related to delays, work missed or exaggerated skills.

Some people believe that some lies are necessary to maintain social interaction. In some cases, recourse to dissimulation can be considered a sign of education, since often the bare truth tends to be interpreted as rudeness. Researchers conducted about two hundred interviews with different types of people, and from there they established profiles and behaviors typical of liars. The conclusion was that men and women lie in the same proportion. While women tend to lie by reference to accidents or sad facts of their lives, men usually have advantages. Many increases or invent professional, personal and sexual achievements.

In some cases, recourse to dissimulation can be considered a sign of education, since often the bare truth tends to be interpreted as rudeness. Lies is, to the human mind, a great weapon of social preservation. From the psychological point of view, lying is an instinctive act of preservation, just as pain or fever are physiological. Without it, society would collapse. Imagine a husband who has many friends and usually makes decisions about how to use his free time. If the woman does not want to accompany him, he can use any excuse, such as working until later, to get rid of the commitment, without hurting those who love him, "he exemplifies.

Lying Is Learned in Childhood

Disguising techniques are often learned by children early on. An example is when parents rebuke their child's frustration at receiving a gift that did not please him. Those responsible often force the child to thank them when they notice some disappointment in the child. And this can be considered a way of stimulating social lies.

Nothing justifies a lie, whatever its intention. And children need to be taught to always tell the truth. This learning happens progressively throughout childhood and parents are the main masters. Children look much more in their attitudes than in their words. Parents who always use truth, who take responsibility for what they do and say, create responsible and ethical children. You only teach yourself what you are.

Recognize A Lie

According to the electronic security expert, few people are prepared to identify a liar on a day-to-day basis. It takes training and practice to improve the ability to "read" the signs of lying. The practitioner teaches that in order to recognize concealment of the truth one must understand the person's standard behavior, pay attention to what he says, the small movements of the face (micro facial expressions), the body and the variations in the tone of the voice.

Our brain does not accept denial. When one lies, one is denying the truth, and some part of one's facial or body expression will denounce it. Aspects such as blink frequency, use of the eyebrows to emphasize some part of the conversation, the position of the hands and legs, stiffness of the shoulder, and aspect of the forehead and mouth are some examples of attitudes that can denounce the lie.

To help you identify a liar, we listed below 8 simple observation tips. Check out:

Lips: Biting or licking lips can be a strong hint of lying.

Voice: those who mind get the vocal cords more stretched than normal, leaving the voice thinner and fainter. To compensate, the person tries to speak louder.

Look: the liar looks away as he tells his lie and then looks closely, wanting to see if he has been able to cheat.

Dryness: Due to an adrenaline reaction, the liar gets a dry mouth and throat, and it is common to choke or swallow dry.

Partially cover the mouth: it translates into a desire to gag. It tends to be a quick gesture because it expresses a conflict: a part of the liar does not want to shut up - but continue with his lie.

Touch the nose: in moments of tension the sensitivity of the nasal mucosa increases. Thus, when lying, the nose itches, although it may be a sensation so soft that barely notice.

Shoulder: Raise one shoulder slightly.

Fake facial expression: When we are genuine, we use the right facial muscles to express an emotion. In a moderate and false smile, the crow's feet do not appear, the cheeks are not lifted and the eyes are less tight. In a real smile, more muscles are used and the upper eyelid bends slightly over the eyes.

If you still cannot identify a lie, try doing the opposite: and encourage the speaker to speak the truth. The tip is to establish closeness in the conversation. The closer you are physical, the more difficulty the person will have to lie.

Insecurity

Insecurity is an emotional state that arises following a situation that is perceived as alarming or threatening. If the person confronted with this stimulus feels that their resources or skills are insufficient to manage and/or overcome the situation, they are likely to feel insecure. This emotion may manifest itself in the form of higher levels of anxiety, psychomotor agitation, allowing the person to feel unnerved but still able to mobilize extra resources to enable him to succeed. In these cases, insecurity has a protective effect in that it prevents us from making mistakes or taking unnecessary risks. For example, when one of the couples feels that their relationship is not safe, they can implement some strategies that, in their eyes, imply the solidification of the relationship, such as the promotion of dialogue, romantic outings or even psychotherapeutic follow-up. Similarly, when a worker perceives his or her place as being at risk of being laid off, he or she will seek alternatives to avoid unemployment. But both in one context and the other insecurity can assume a higher level of intensity, no longer having such protective effect.

In these cases, though is likely to be dominated by irrational beliefs, which grow spirally and produce a blocking effect. The person starts to live by what makes him insecure without, however, being able to find adjusted solutions. In the first example, this state of anxiety could translate into a set of behaviors that have both despair and nonsense, such as starting to search the partner's cell for signs of a potential extramarital relationship, aggressive and/or controlling comments, etc. In the following example, it could happen that the person would be so depressed that he would not invest either in the current job or in the search for the new placement, allowing insecurity to have the blocking effect.

What clues or signs are evidenced by someone who is insecure? How can we identify him?

The most insecure people are overwhelmed by fear, and as a result, it is usually more difficult for them to take an assertive stance, that is, they have very serious difficulties in expressing clearly and honestly what they think and what they feel. Within a group, both can strive to go unnoticed as they can make efforts to please everyone. In practice, they feel an intense fear of failing, of not meeting expectations, of not being up to it. There are people who are very confident in professional terms and who are more insecure in relational/affective terms. In the same way, there are people who feel safe and comfortable in the performance of roles related to effective relationships but which reveal serious insecurities in other areas of life. It may not be easy to recognize the most insecure people, especially if the analysis is superficial.

Sometimes it is easier for an insecure person to recognize another who shares the same insecurities, as he is more aware and more attentive to certain details that will go along with the majority.

Are We Born Insecure or Does It Come as We Grow Up?

Our personality is largely conditioned by our experiences from childhood. To the extent that a child is able to build secure emotional bonds with the adults around them, the likelihood of becoming a self-confident adult increase. But even so, some traumatic events or some adult affective relationships can be shocking enough to shake this self-confidence.

For example, a person may be able to be assertive and emotionally intelligent during their development and into adulthood to experience one or two experiences in which he or she is betrayed (by the loving partner or close friends) and see their safety severely shaken from so. Of course, the stronger our emotional baggage, the more likely we are to take a resilient stance in these circumstances. In other words, there is a kind of "savings," which are nothing more than all the affective ties that have contributed to the structuring of our personality, which can help us to more quickly overcome a potentially traumatic situation, the sleeves and preventing us from feeding feelings of insecurity. For the rest, people with solid emotional bonds tend to be safer people.

How Can This Feeling Hurt Us? How Does Insecurity Affect or Limit Our Lives?

As I mentioned before, to the extent that insecurity and anxiety take over our lives can become disabling. When this emotion takes over us, we begin to feel incapable and to live by negative thoughts that have little or nothing to be reasonable.

Are There Advantages in Feeling Insecure? If So, Which Ones?

As I mentioned before, in certain "doses" insecurity can be protective, functioning as a defense mechanism that causes our internal alarm to sound and force us to act. From the moment it becomes overwhelming, insecurity has no advantage.

How Can We Deal with And Overcome Insecurity? What Strategies Can We Use?

First and foremost, let us assume that we depend on social and affective ties, either because they foster our self-esteem and sense of support, or because social interactions are the only way for our most irrational thoughts to be disrupted. As fear and insecurity grow, it is expected that the ruminations, the negative thoughts that are easily transformed, in our eyes, into insurmountable ghosts will also flourish. Solid integration into a (real) support social network is half way for some of these ghosts to be deconstructed and we can see the light at the bottom of the tunnel, even in the most catastrophic scenarios.

But our support network - family members, colleagues, and friends - may not be enough to help us in times of deep crisis and/or when our insecurity reaches a character of chronicity. Insofar as we feel that our life does not evolve because insecurity does not allow it, it is time to resort to psychotherapeutic help in order to identify the source of the vulnerabilities and acquire the skills to stop the vicious cycles.

Is There Any Kind of Therapy or Treatment That Can Be Done? If Yes, What and What Does It Consist? What Aspects Are Worked On?

In therapy, each case is unique and special. I cannot label an unsafe person, and from there, apply a stereotyped therapeutic plan. There are, however, some common procedures in these cases, which almost always go through the analysis of the life history of each person and their respective identification of what I call the cycles of vulnerability, that is, the relat onal patterns that cause the behaviors. Then it is necessary to invest in the development of social skills, which includes assertiveness training, that is, specific tools are shared, that the person is applying with attempts and errors, experiencing behaviors alternative to those with which he is familiar and, of course, also obtaining return different that nourishes the will to continue to change.

What is the solution to the following scenarios of insecurity: you cannot ask for what you want, nor defend your wants and needs; It costs you to speak in public; the criticisms paralyze it; does not feel good about your body; does not know how to accept/deal with compliments; your self-esteem is in bad shape; he does not know how to express his disagreement; have difficulty meeting and socializing with new people; insecurity in love relationships; after the birth of the first child, some men complain that women no longer pay attention to them and only care about the baby?

Most of these situations have one element in common: the lack of assertiveness, that is, the ability to assume a position clearly and honestly. But this is maybe, just the tip of the iceberg. If it is possible to implement an assertiveness training that helps one to be firmer, assuming what one feels or thinks, it is essential to carry out a deeper analysis and to identify the origin of each vulnerability. There are old wounds that may need healing, and this requires a specific therapeutic path for each person.

In Addition to These Situations, What Are the Most Common Insecurities and How Can We Overcome Them? (Concrete Examples)

The most common fears are related to what our greatest needs are. We need to feel secure in affective terms, we need them to like us, we need them to value us (both from a personal point of view and from a professional point of view). To the extent that any of these needs take time to be satisfied, it increases the probability of feeding unreasonable ideas about what we are capable of, of what we are worth or of what others think of us and of behaving fear-ridden.

How to Find Out When Someone Is Lying by Text Message

WhatsApp, Messenger, emails and even the old SMS' are used nowadays for more instantaneous communication. But can you tell when someone is lying by text message when they use these features?

Although many people find this type of conversation the safest way to get through that ill-told lie, the truth is that it is possible to find out when someone is lying by text message. And most important of all: it is not so difficult to identify signs of lies in these messages.

Today, for example, you will learn some signs that clearly indicate when someone is lying by text message, for whatever reason. The tips we've listed below are a summary of the research done.

How to Find Out When Someone Is Lying in A Text Message:

1. Long Sentences

Unlike face-to-face conversations, where people tend to use more personal pronouns and elaborate vague and shorter phrases when someone is lying by text message to tendency is to write more.

In most lying messages, the researchers noted that both men and women use this feature, albeit unconsciously. In their case, the messages usually get up to 13% longer. In their case, sentences increase by an average of 2%.

2. Words that do not compromise

Another common thing to notice when you are lying by text message is the use of non-compromising phrases and words, such as "probably, possibly, maybe."

3. Impersonality

Phrases and attitudes of detachment can also be a clue to lies. The impersonal tone, for example, suggests that he or she does not feel close to you and this is already a point that helps their lie.

4. Evasive Answers

When you ask something straight and you get an inconsistent answer, which does not answer anything, it can also be a lie. Pay attention to the tone adopted in this type of situation.

5. Excessive caution

Repeated cautionary expressions may also be a sign that honesty is lacking in the message. "To be honest," "there's nothing to worry about" and "I'm sorry to say" are some vague, over-cautious expressions that people often use when they lie as they type a message.

6. Sudden change of verbal tense

Stories that begin to be told in the past and which, from nowhere, are counted in the present and vice versa. When someone changes the verbal tense of narration suddenly, it can be a lie.

Narrations of what happens, in general, are made in the past. However, if the person is inventing a story, the sentences tend to come out in the present, since it is easier for the brain to follow up on what is being said.

7. Inconsistent Stories

When someone types a lying message and tells inconsistent stories, they are probably lying. It is common for the liar himself to lose himself in the details and end up contradicting himself after a while, for example, leaving the story told with inconsistent spaces.

How to Make Your Child Stop Lying?

Do you know why your child lies? Do you know when he's lying? Here we will talk about it and give you suggestions on how to stop the lying. Early education is important that will help not to prolong bad habits during adulthood. Being an honest person promotes a good social life, in addition to keeping friends and family always around.

Lies worry a lot of moms and dads who do not know what to do because they think the child is too naive to understand what they are doing. But it is good to understand that if young people are not taught early on that lying is wrong, they will continue to do it all the time, and this can worsen over time, to the point where they will no longer know what is true and what is not.

Why Do Children Lie?

Children often lie for the same reasons as adults, but the main motivation is that lying is often easier than telling the truth. Check out the most common situations:

They Are in Trouble

Like when you see your child wet and ask "Was it you who wet the whole house?" This is a question that you already know the answer to. So, the child feels pressured to lie. Instead, try saying that you know that it was he or she who did it and that they have to help undo it by showing that there are consequences for what happened.

Feel Threatened / Afraid of Being Punished

They know that they have done something wrong and that they will receive a punishment, so they lie to avoid punishment. Try to talk to them and explain the situation instead of simply punishing.

So That Others Accept Them

This often happens with older children, who feel the need to invent things that make it seem cooler to their colleagues. This can be improved by teaching your child that people will like him for the way they are and not the way they pretend to be.

Follow the Example of The Parents

If parents lie, they are teaching children that this attitude is right. So, there's no point of berating the little one when you have set a wrong example.

Signs That Your Child Is Lying

Avoiding / Excessive Eye Contact

Little ones tend to avoid eye contact at the time of lying, but elder ones do the opposite, fixing their eyes on the opposite person. Both these situations indicate the fact that the story being told is false.

Repetition

A very common act is to repeat the question at the time of responding, so the child has more time to think of an answer.

Inconsistencies

When the child speaks one thing and then contradicts himself, it is a sign that he is lying. The child is probably making up the story at the time and what he tells may make no sense at all.

Defensive Reactions

It is normal for the child to be defensive when accused of doing something bad, but if this defense is too much, be suspicious.

Unusual gestures

Look for unusual gestures in your child when he is telling a story. If he keeps his hands still or uses his hands too much while talking, he is trying to divert his attention from the problem. It is a sign that what he is saying is not true.

Blinking too much or too little

Nervousness at the time of lying makes the child blink too much while talking or sometimes they make even forget to blink.

Not Being Quiet

Your child is restless, moving his hands, feet and squirming as if he wanted to pee. This is a sign that what he is telling may not be true and therefore he is uncomfortable. This is his body's way of rejecting the lies.

Gossiping

If your child is already talkative, you will have a harder time noticing this sign, but if he is not you will realize that he will start talking without stopping, trying to make you believe the lie by adding details.

Change the Way They Speak

Speaking too keenly, hesitating, and pausing to think indicates that the child is not being true.

How Do We End the Lies?

Do not ask your child to lie. As we said above, the child follows the example of adults, so asking him to answer the phone and tell him you're not home only encourages him to do more. There are many small things that parents tend to tell their children to do without realizing it can become a habit.

Teach the child that the mistakes he or she makes are opportunities to learn and they do not need to be hidden. They can lie and they should not be afraid to disappoint you with the truth. Explain that they are loved even when they are wrong because even you, as parents, sometimes make mistakes but that does not give you a reason to hide things. Try and set the right example and always speak the truth. Also, reward your child when they speak the truth because recognition will encourage them to be honest in the future as well.

Chapter 10 - Danger Signals

Scientists have concluded that personalities are generally divided into envious, pessimistic, confident and optimistic. Teamwork can be conclusive proof of your personality type. Every person is a world, or so they say. Although people who have gone through several companies know that, for one reason or another, it seems that certain patterns repeat themselves. If people divided into groups, depending on how they react to different situations, would you know how to recognize each of them?

Game Theory

To analyze these social behaviors, a study was based on the so-called "game theory". A researcher in this study said, "game theory is a mathematical way of approaching situations in which two or more people have to make decisions that affect everyone". This idea is based on the idea that all people know in advance the consequences of their decisions and therefore will act in their own interest.

According to the study, which viewed the responses of over 500 volunteers to various social dilemmas, game theory can be applied to identify different patterns of personalities. One of the most well-known games of this theory is called a "prisoner's dilemma," which shows that two people may not cooperate, even if this goes against their interest.

The researcher explains that the best way to understand the game is through a concrete example: "Suppose you and I have to do a job that must be evaluated by a boss. Each of us has to make a choice between two options: striving and helping one another, or not acting and letting the other do everything." In this case, the options would be: to divide the efforts between the two; that one strives and the other does not; or that, finally, nobody does anything, considering that in this case neither would receive for the work.

Continuing with the example, there were four very different groups. On the one hand, the envious, "who are those who, when interacting with another person, prefer to earn less, if in this way make sure to earn more than the other person," meaning that they could boycott work; the other group is that of optimists, that is, "those who seek the maximum gain, supposing, therefore, that the decision of the other will be the one that will allow them to achieve", so that you can be seated because you will be the other who will do all the work; the opposite of these would be the pessimists, "who think that the other will come to annoy them, and therefore try to pass an image that is the least bad possible," so they strive to do the work, thinking that the other will not do; and finally, there would be the confident, that is, "the good people who make the decision that would lead to a better outcome for all (though not the best for them individually)." This was one of the examples, although the idea was to offer volunteers different social games of this style, recording what kinds of decisions they made in each of them.

There Are More Envious People

Analyzing the sample, the results revealed that 20% of the people corresponded to an optimistic profile, another 20% to a pessimistic profile, 20% were in the trust group and 30% belonged to the envy block. Another 10%, however, did not meet the established standards, since they seemed to choose by chance.

If it is possible to draw any conclusion from this study, then it would be true that the envious are more. With the classification in groups we see (and we would like other experiments to confirm), one might think that when we go out on the street, we have a 30% chance to run into an envious person, 20% find an optimist, and so on , and try to make decisions based on this information.

Although the researchers make it clear that this is a very theoretical study and that people do not work that way, because when we find an unknown, which would be the closest to the experiment, we do not know which it's your type; so it's not easy to take that into account to interact with it. The idea they actually let air up is that "if for some reason we interact repeatedly with the same person, we can begin to understand their personality and use that information for our own decisions."

Recognizing and Interacting with Each Type of Personality

The question to ask is how we recognize these personalities or what we should focus on to classify them. Perhaps the most important thing is to recognize the envious because they are dangerous people. We must not forget that, after all, being willing to have fewer benefits to stay above the other is highly destructive behavior, and worse, not only to the other but to the envious one himself. To recognize them, he adds that "it is best to focus precisely on the attention given to what others can attain when interacting with them."

Regarding the optimists and pessimists, researchers report that "in our study, we also see behaviors that are associated with very different perceptions of risk: so, the optimists are very willing to risk, while the pessimists are completely the opposite."

So "if we see that someone behaves in a crazy way, it's quite likely to be an optimist"; on the contrary, people overly cautious and who tend to inactivity and excuses could respond to a pessimistic profile. However, we should not confuse ourselves with the positive character of the former and negative of the seconds, since "with both, you have to be cautious, because depending on the situation we share, decisions can be bad for us." So, going no further, in the example given by game theory, "the optimist would not work, so we had better do the work."

Chapter 11 - Facial Expression

Microexpressions are very fast and involuntary facial expressions that are produced as a manifestation of an emotion that we are feeling. I will tell you a secret: they let us know what the person we are relating to is feeling since they are innate and universal in character.

Learning to identify them will facilitate your personal relationships, improving the expression of your emotions and, with that, your needs and also those of your partner, friend, family, etc. ... on the other hand, very useful advice to know what the other person is feeling is imitated your facial expression.

This trick allows us to understand that by manipulating our body language we can experience any emotional response we desire. That is, we have the incredible power to generate emotions through our expression.

How Many Facial Expressions Are There?

To date, more than 10,000 different facial expressions have been cataloged, with only 7 basic micro expressions being identified.

Universal and subtle gestures that allow us to read emotions in the countenance of the person we are looking at and form the basis of the rest of the facial expressions.

The 7 basic micro expressions are constituted by:

Anger. The micro-expression of anger focuses mainly on the upper part of the face, where we lower and raise eyebrows, frowning. We tend to tighten and tighten our mouths, gently separating our lips and gritting our teeth. A gesture of anger itself is to point the chin forward in a challenging way.

The fear. This microexpression is characterized by tense eyebrows and wide-open eyes so that we can see everything we can see in our visual field since we are perceiving danger somewhere. In the lower part of the face, the jaw is loose, and it is also an instinctive behavior to allow us to scream and take the air.

The joy. Joy is demonstrated with bright eyes and wrinkles at its outer ends and lower eyelids. One trick: when a person feigns joy, these wrinkles are not formed. We will also show the characteristic smile, which the more joyful we feel, the more we open our teeth.

The contempt. In this expression, the upper part of the face can adopt different gestures, and the secret to identifying it is in the lower part of the face; since we express a very particular expression that consists of raising one side of the mouth, forming a half smile.

After research on this microexpression, it has been proven that thanks to it, one can know if a marriage will end in a divorce; if this gesture of contempt is usually between the two people.

The surprise. It is characterized by raised and arched eyebrows, with very open eyes. In the lower part of the face, the jaw will be loose and the mouth open.

The sadness. This is one of the most complicated micro-expressions to pretend. It is characterized by low eyebrows that meet, subtly, in the center. Usually, the mouth is arched down.

Aversion. This microexpression is one of the easiest to identify since the whole expression is concentrated between the mouth and the nose. The nose s wrinkled and the upper lip is raised, often leaving the upper teeth in view. We also show it in personal relationships when we feel disapproved or when we do not like someone.

NEGATIVE PERSONALITY ADJECTIVES

aggressive	discourteous	mysterious
angry	disobedient	nervous
apathetic	disloyal	obnoxious
aimless	embarrassed	offensive
aloof	fanatical	panicky
amoral	fanciful	picky
annoying	fawning	pitiful
argumentative	fickle	repulsive
arrogant	fierce	rude
bewildered	frivolous	scary
big-headed	goody-goody	smarty-pants
blunt	grumpy	smart aleck
bossy	helpless	spoilsport
clingy	indecisive	tactless
clumsy	impulsive	thoughtless
conceited	jealous	unpleasant
crafty	killjoy	uptight
crude	know-it-all	wise guy
cynical	lazy	worried
defeated	materialistic	

Facial Expression: Your Face Says It All

Psychologists say that any of us can recognize the faces of other people basic human emotions. Humans are different from each other, but identical in the way they express their emotions. Studies indicate that it is possible to know when someone is happy, sad or distressed - or when he is pretending all this.

Anyone, anywhere on the planet, can recognize the elemental emotions on the face of another person: fear, surprise, anger, disgust, sadness, anguish, and joy. The face is the main place where our emotions express themselves. As we are all, after all, deeply visual creatures, facial expressions become a universal language.

Why Is It Important to Know How to Identify Emotions? How Can This Help Us in Practical Life?

When identifying the expressions of emotion, one can, for example, perceive when a person is lying. In the celebrated episode involving President Bill Clinton with his trainee, it was very clear that he was not telling the truth. He not only had lie expressions on his face but also used the expression "that woman" to refer to Monica Lewinsky. One of the things people do when they lie is to use the language of detachment. We all knew Clinton knew Monica. Still, he referred to her as "that woman."

When Someone Tries to Hide Their Emotions (For Example, Smiling When Sad), Is There Any Way To "Read" The Face and Know the Real Feeling of The Person?

Yes. When a muscle located in the area of the eyebrow rises slightly, it reveals that the person is sad. If you realize this detail, you will know that the person is sad even before they know it. Another example: to give a false smile, the person moves only the muscles that go from the chin to the corner of the lip. To give a genuine smile, generated by genuine emotion, the person moves those same muscles and also others around the eyes which are practically impossible to command.

The smile of Mona Lisa has already been analyzed by a computer. She would express 83% of happiness, 9% of disgust, 6% of fear and 2% of irritation.

Mona Lisa is an interesting case because it mainly involves the lips. As for facial expression, Mona Lisa's head is turned to one side and her gaze is directed slightly to the other side. This is one of the things that happen during a flirtation: there is a discreet smile, you look to one side to see someone and then look back at the same place. I would say, therefore, that Mona Lisa has a flirtatious look.

Chapter 12 - Eye Reading

What Can the Format of Your Eyes Reveal About Your Personality?

Many believe that our eyes are the window of the soul. Through the eyes, it is possible to perceive emotions and to pass messages even without having to use any words.

What we have not yet talked about, and a lot of people do not know, is that the shape of their eyes can have a lot to say about their personality traits. Chinese people specializing in facial reading have been able, after years of research, to establish connections between the various formats and characteristics of people.

Deep Eyes

People with the deepest eyes also indicate a personality with the same tendency. They are more observant people who like to research and analyze everything around them. In addition, they are usually smart and insightful.

Rounded eyes

Those who have the most circular shaped eye tend to show their feelings openly, rather than keeping them hidden. They are expressive, dramatic and impulsive people.

Away Eyes

If someone has their eyes slightly further from the center of the face than the ordinary, they can be a more carefree, adventurous, and always willing to try new and different things, even if they seem strange.

Close Eyes

Despite having the opposite format of the eyes away, does not indicate necessarily opposing personalities. People with closest eyes are energetic and stubborn.

Amber Eyes

In this eye shape, the outer corner is slightly raised, which may indicate passionate but calm people with their feet on the ground.

Eyes Inclined Downward

This type of eye shape may indicate pessimism. Despite this, it also represents very loyal and fellow people.

Eyes Inclined Upward

People with these eyes have a tendency to have focus and guidance in life, and they are not accustomed to accepting any response to any situation.

Small Eyes

Small-eyed people often repair small details in things more easily and are thorough and perfectionist.

Encapsulated Eyes

This eye type keeps the moving eyelid hidden. People who possess it are usually very calm and deal with things and situations in life with an open mind.

Leading Eyes

The projected eyelids give the impression that the eye is larger, as is the sensitivity of the people who have them. Those who have this eye shape have a tendency to prefer to be in smaller groups of people.

What Is the Shape of Your Eye? Did You Identify Yourself with The Characteristics Placed?

Chapter 13 - Handwriting

What does your handwriting say about you?

The traits with which the graphic analysis is done in the Human Resources area is amazing. Some experts believe that graphology - personality analysis based on handwriting - can be a useful ally in candidate selection. According to experts, graphology allows identifying about 300 traits of character, including some that other techniques do not distinguish.

On the other hand, starting from a more "natural" exercise that most of us have in their daily lives since the 6/7 years, it effectively reduces the tension associated with all evaluation processes, with beneficial results for candidates and active professionals.

In this sense, and by allowing a deeper knowledge of a professional, the study of handwriting may be relevant in recruitment, selection, training, and career development.

We were able to know what traces the graphological analysis in the area of Human Resources.

Graphical analysis does not take into account the fact that the letter is beautiful or ugly or the fact that the author is Dextrose or left-handed. The study focuses exclusively on handwriting and not on ancillary issues.

However, issues such as the direction of the text, spacing of letters and lines and the way space is used, are aspects of great importance in an analysis of this type.

For it to be more reliable, it is important that the text to be analyzed is at least 20 lines, written on an unpublished white sheet and the person is not aware that it is being tested.

Concrete Aspects of The Graphological Analysis:

The signature is one of the most relevant elements in this type of evaluation. For example, if people with average self-esteem do not make any kind of underlining, an underline signature already demonstrates that this is a self-confident person with above-average self-esteem. On the other hand, the person who feels the need to mark his / her signature with various traits, either in the form of

underlining or accessory elements to the name, is probably very insecure and with low self-esteem.

Another element very characteristic in this analysis are letters like the letter T, with a high degree of personalization. If the upper bar of the letter "t" is made only on the right side, we may be facing a very emotional person with difficulty controlling emotions and eventually in relationships with others. When the "t" bar crosses the center, this person probably does not have a bad temper.

The bond given to the letters in each word is also a distinctive personality factor in writing. If it is customary to chain the letters with no space between them, it is probably a person with a reasonably logical and rational reasoning and fast thinking. On the other hand, who, in each word, makes a large spacing between letters, almost pushing them apart, tends to be an insecure, unconfident person.

Already the spacing between words, when very large, indicates a need for freedom and valorization of autonomy in the accomplishment of the work. People who practically do not leave spaces between words, like to be accompanied.

Also, the way the role of space is harnessed translates important traits of our personality. To leave a few margins in the text and to tend to use the sheet until the end, shows impatience and great impulsivity. On the other hand, a very centered text, with very similar short spaces between right, left, upper and lower margin reveals that the author plans things in advance.

Still in the distribution of space, if the left margin is too large, there is a great orientation for the future and desire to see "things to go". On the contrary, if the right margin is very large there is a direction for the past, I am afraid.

As for letter form, it is usually associated with the care that people give to the activities they are engaged in or how they react to the stimuli they receive. Around letter are a sign of care, attention, and precision, kindness and generosity. The very angular letters demonstrate, in turn, self-discipline, rigidity, and analytical thinking. Open, incomplete letters denounce a person who talks a lot, and who may have difficulty keeping secrecy on certain issues.

The direction the text takes, more inclined to the left or right, for example, can tell a lot about how a person deals with emotions. Tilt to

the left is usually associated with shyness, withdrawal, or a person very attached to the emotions, resistant to change because of being too attached to the past. An inclination to the right, in the opposite direction, is linked to extroversion, the balance between emotion and reason, expressiveness, orientation towards the future, and sociability. Perpendicular writing (without gradient) usually identifies well-balanced and fairly objective personalities.

If, when writing on an "imaginary line," the person can maintain a straight line, it is possibly a personality that is rigid and demanding, but that knows how to get to the heart of the issues and with a great capacity for self-motivation. If the line goes down, it will be an indicator of some weariness or pessimism, perhaps even a penchant for discouragement in the face of obstacles. Upward lines already point to a lot of energy, optimism, and ambition.

The way the text appears, very erased, normal or very dense, can denounce the mood of its author. A strong pressure, shows determination, some aggression and take things seriously. Already a text almost erased shows timidity, but can also be a sign of some laziness or lack of energy, sadness.

Relative to letter size, when small indicates caution, concentration, modesty, and some intolerance. The medium-sized letter reveals an easily adaptable, practical and realistic person. On the other hand, great letter manifests extroversion, leadership, generosity, and lack of attention to details.

The dot in the "I" - when placed close to the letter demonstrates attention to detail. Sometimes over the dash, other times beside it means that it is more attentive to some details than to others. Without a point, it means that it gives little attention to detail, which can be careless or overlooked.

When the "e" curve is very much the same, the person in question knows how to be a good listener and tolerant of the ideas and behavior of others. The "open" we can be too tolerant, accepting the point of view of others without question. The very closed "e" has his opinion and is very complicated to understand the point of view of other people.

If you end the words in a curve pointing up and to the left is by nature a person who likes to be in the spotlight. If it ends without curves, it does not need the approval of the others.

If the second curve of the "m" is as high as the second, do not have major concerns about how it is seen by others. If the second curve is higher than the first curve, it is concerned with what others think and does not want to have any objectionable behavior. If the second curve is lower than the first, it indicates diplomacy.

Chapter 14 - Human Cognition

In order to characterize the role of the cognitive psychologist in the space of Psychology as a science and profession, this chapter will address some aspects related to the relation of cognitive psychology within Psychology itself, reflecting on the performance of the cognitive psychologist as a scientist and professional, looking for the role of professionals in related areas.

Some historical aspects related to the emergence of cognitive psychology will be considered in order to better characterize the way in which it was defined and how it was positioned in the face of some theoretical and methodological presuppositions in force after the Second World War. In fact, in the last decades, the study of cognitive processes has expanded rapidly and, from the theoretical point of view, has been shown to be a relevant approach to the explanation of human behavior, bringing to the fore central aspects of psychology.

The aspects emphasized here are more than answers, generating reflections and questions, contributing to a greater understanding of the cognitive area within psychology as a whole.

Historical Considerations: From Behaviorism to Cognitive psychology, as well as other areas of psychology, has been negatively influenced by a series of restrictive assumptions defined as positivists. These presuppositions specified that the object of study of psychology would be exclusively the observable behavior and that the correct way of carrying out investigations on this object would be through the determination of the stimulus-response relationship, that is, through the search for correlations between conditions general external to the individual) and the responses given by the individual to these conditions. Within this approach, the study of behavior was limited to the identification of the correlations between the variables as a function of the experimental context and the observable responses in the behaviors produced by the individual. What happens inside the individual was, in fact, irrelevant and eliminated from the investigation, since such aspects could not be adequately controlled.

These presuppositions were rejected by cognitive psychology, which sought to overcome this reductionist and mechanistic model of behavior, assuming that it is not possible to treat the relationship between the stimulus and the response as simple and linear. In this approach, attention is focused on the structures, processes, and mechanisms that constitute the mind of the individual, the same mind that had been dismissed by behaviorists and metaphorically defined as the "Black Box."

This refusal to accept the ER model, preached by the behaviorists, started from the evidence that in the individual there are mechanisms and processes that will take action at the time of the elicitation of the answers, independently of the level of simplicity or elaboration of these. As underlined by researchers, in the course of psychological investigation it is impossible to abstract the conditions of the complex functioning of the individual which, in his way of operating, influences not only the response, that is, the final product of behavior, but also has a retroactive effect on the intensity and quality of the stimulus.

In this way, cognitive psychology considers the linear model ER limiting, insufficient and consequently inadequate to explain human behavior, seeking to replace it with a more complex and elaborate scheme that considers in a circular way this dyadic relationship between organism and stimuli. The organization has a relevant and active role, a system capable of complex elaborations, such as: making choices among the relevant elements of a given situation, using alternative strategies, selectively storing information, performing transformations on the elements in order to elaborate them, and

In this way, the cognitive psychologist's task is to discover laws that establish connections between the behavior and the variety of cognitive psychology. aspects and elements with which the behavior is related to address the problem more comprehensively. On the epistemological and methodological plane, this task includes the elaboration of theoretical models of the structures of the processes and the mechanisms that constitute the mental life of the individual. The study of conditions that influence behavior thus becomes only a means to this end. In other words, psychology has to try to go beyond the simple establishment of certain behaviors that manifest themselves under certain conditions but to seek to elaborate explanatory models of the broader mechanisms that operate in the mind of the subject, on the basis of which the individual manifests that behavior in those conditions.

The parallelism established between the human organism and computer points out that the task of the cognitive psychologist, who seeks to understand the mechanisms and processes in the acquisition and development of knowledge, is analogous to that of the computer technician who seeks to discover how computer. For example, in the case of a program for storing information, the technician has to find out through which procedures this goal is achieved. It does not matter at all if the computer stores the information on a floppy disk, hard disk, or magnetic tape, which is really important is to understand the program and not the computer itself.

The program is a set of assertions expressed in a particular language that constitute the instructions the computer has to execute to process a series of symbols of type "if the stimulus is of type X, perform 'X' operations, but if the stimulus is of Y-type, perform 'Y' operations ... process the combinations of the various inputs in this way and ... etc. Thus, the cognitive psychologist seeks to achieve explanations of this kind for all mechanisms, aiming to discover how information is developed within the human body.

Anyway, cognitive psychology is not concerned with the elaboration of stimulation conditions that produce a particular behavior, or to indicate just how likely it is possible to elicit a certain response from certain stimulation. On the contrary, it seeks to specify the mechanisms and mental processes in the organism and to propose models that indicate the phases of the mental processes and the functions developed by these phases.

Following these historical considerations, it is necessary to present what we understand by cognitive psychology, its relation with other areas of psychology and related areas, comparing, also, different perspectives on cognitive psychology around the world.

Cognitive Psychology: Object and form of Research

Psychology is a science that is present in several areas: social, affective-emotional, pathological, educational, in work relations and in the cognitive area. Most people, especially those who are not directly attached to psychology, believe that psychologists work only as therapists and that they probably have some "special gift" to get to know people deeply. However, we know that there are several areas in psychological science and one of them is the cognitive point of reflection in this work.

The Cognitive Psychologist's Research Object

The cognitive psychologist studies the bases of human knowledge; more precisely, it studies the means by which the individual reaches an organized knowledge of the world into categories, as well as the way in which this knowledge is used to direct and plan actions on the environment. This categorized knowledge becomes indispensable as an instrument of understanding and acting on reality.

Researchers state that the world of each individual's experience is made up of an enormous number of different objects, events, people, and impressions capable of being discriminated and categorized in an organized manner by the individual. If individuals did not have this ability to record differences and categorize them into an organized world, they would probably be overwhelmed by the complexity of the environment.

Thus, the cognitive psychologist studies not only how external information is extracted, but especially how this information is conceptualized and organized internally so that it can be used effectively. We may also add that he is concerned with aspects that imply internal elaborations, based on the assumption that the response to the given stimulus situation has undergone some elaboration within the individual, and that this elaboration does not depend only on the external stimulus presented, but of internal mental processes present in the mind of the individual at a certain moment of its development and in function of previous elaborations that have been affected.

Using more traditional terminology, the cognitive psychologist studies aspects of cognitive activity represented by perception, memory, mental image, though, reasoning, learning, etc. In other words, one is interested in the mental mechanisms that act when one perceives, memories, mentally elaborate a given object, when one learns, and so on. These contents of consciousness are considered as the product of a series of elaborations and operations conducted on and from information and which refer to knowledge.

The Cognitive Psychologist's Way of Studying

We have seen that the interest of cognitive psychology lies in the nature of knowledge, in the structures and processes by which it is acquired, and in the way in which it develops. This interest translates into experimental studies, for in fact it does not study the basis of knowledge from speculations, but through empirical studies, like any other scientist.

For this, observation becomes an instrument of fundamental importance. According to studies, learning to observe in psychology is somewhat more difficult than one thinks and requires us to try to find the meanings of behavior in observation, seeking to abandon our particular perspective and to discover the world's perspective of the subject in observation, its mode to operate on the environment and the meanings it attributes to people and things. However, observation in itself, however trustworthy, cannot be viewed in isolation, and it is necessary to establish a relation between observing, reflecting and understanding.

Having established this relationship, the cognitive psychologist raises hypotheses, testing them, seeking to understand the phenomena that he proposes to investigate. In this sense, his work closely resembles the work of the scientist in the investigation of the aspects of knowledge, and may often be used of research methods such as the clinical method, for example (Note D) or methods derived from other areas such as Anthropology.

Cognitive Psychology and other areas of Psychology

By analyzing the role of cognitive psychology, we must reflect on its status within Psychology itself. Considering the emphasis historically given to clinical psychology, for a long time the role of the psychologist related only to the care and treatment of personal problems related to affective-emotional aspects. Undoubtedly this is a relevant area of Psychology, as are the other areas as well.

Putting clinical psychology and cognitive psychology in perspective, what we can see at the moment is a sectorization in the domain of knowledge. The cognitive psychologist does not know much about affective-emotional aspects, information that even though not being relevant to the level of his scientific production as a researcher, would be important at the practical level. The clinical psychologist, in turn, discards information about cognitive development from his praxis.

Take a hypothetical example the case of a child who has learning difficulties. In the view of the cognitive psychologist, these difficulties can be attributed aprioristically to problems in the scope of cognitive development. In the view of the clinical psychologist, these same difficulties will undoubtedly be attributed to personal problems experienced by the child. Both by one professional, alternative hypothesis are immediately discarded from their investigations into the case.

We do not want to state here that it would be up to the cognitive psychologist to deal with the affective-emotional difficulties of the child in question, or that the clinical psychologist, a specialist in affective-emotional difficulties, should develop some kind of cognitive therapy with it. Hence the importance of specialized expertise. But when it comes to sectoral competences, the relevant information is not considered and hypotheses are a priori discarded from the repertoire of possible responses to the case under study.

But beyond the problem of the sectorization of knowledge within psychology itself, cognitive psychology is confronted with the problem of incomprehension of what are cognitive studies and Piagetian studies, and a reflection on this seems to be necessary.

Cognitive Psychology and Related Areas

In an attempt to understand the role of cognitive psychology, it is relevant to analyze the relationship between these and other related areas.

Cognitive psychology refers to the study of knowledge, consequently involves the investigation of topics relevant to education, such as learning, thinking, reasoning, the formation of concepts, memory, intelligence, etc. In this way, the professional practice of the cognitive psychologist is often interrelated with the field of action of other professionals such as those of the educational area.

When the school psychologist adopts a cognitive approach, his / her performance may often be closely related to the pedagogue's performance.

To better understand this interrelationship, it is worth analyzing some aspects that have attracted the attention of the school psychologist. At first, the school psychologist's practice was similar to that of the clinical psychologist, since his attention turned more to the personal aspects related to the individual than to the learning itself. The emphasis of his work was fundamentally on the investigation of interpersonal relations (teacher-student, students among themselves) and on the search for solutions to personal problems that could arise in the school routine or as a consequence of the relations in the school context or as a consequence of the relations in the context that could, in one way or another, affect student learning.

Often the school psychologist's room became, in a sense, a therapeutic practice, especially when the difficulties presented could not be referred to a professional outside the school (as is often the case with school clients from low socio-economic classes).

In part this emphasis is explained by the basically clinical orientation offered by university curricula, adopting practices based on the medical model of individual care. With the changes that have emerged in psychology around the world, and specifically with the advancement of studies in the cognitive area and consequently the insertion of disciplines related to this area in Psychology courses, the focus of attention of the school psychologist turns to the aspects related to cognitive processes in general.

In this way, the attention and performance of the school psychologists are close to the area of activity of the pedagogue. Although such roles should not be confused, it is clear that cognitive psychology is of interest to both of them, and its contribution to the practice of each one should be more clearly defined.

Often when the cognitive psychologist engages in pedagogical problems, from the results of his own research, he tends to raise educational implications without due consideration of the contribution of pedagogy, ar d he may suffer from the problem of providing an overly psychological approach to pedagogical topics and problems.

On the other hand, the pedagogue in an attempt to operationalize the results of psychological research, from an instrumental and even reductionist perspective, tends to abstract the data from the theoretical context in which they are inserted, advocating for themselves the supreme role of organizer and elaborator of these at the level the problem of giving a simplistic focus to complex issues, generalizing conclusions and standardizing procedures.

In order to separate the difficulties implicit in this dichotomy between theory and praxis, it is necessary to consider that both disciplines, with their peculiarities and instances, should interact. This does not mean that the pedagogue has to be more a psychologist or vice versa, but that it is necessary to recognize the existence of specialized skills that, however, should be exchanged to minimize distortions between theory and practice. This is not to say that it is impracticable to transpose the theoretical results of cognitive research into pedagogical praxis, but that this transposition requires joint and interdisciplinary work.

Cognitive Psychology Around the World

Besides the analysis of cognitive psychology within psychology as a whole, other considerations need to be taken into account.

Cognitive psychology is essentially concerned with the study of the processes and structures of human knowledge, not including the study of the development of these structures and processes. Cognitive psychology in the Anglo-Saxon tradition relates to information processing, artificial intelligence; the structure of thought, reasoning, memory, etc. The interest lies in the structure, processing, and functioning of the phenomena of consciousness. In turn, developmental psychology investigates the modifications that such structures, processes, and functioning undergo throughout the development of the individual.

Take any phenomenon, such as perception, for example. In the American tradition, while cognitive psychology would be interested in investigating the basis of human perception, in which it constitutes such a phenomenon, as occurs the perception under this or that circumstance, what influences it, what effect it has on other elements of consciousness, etc.; developmental psychology would be interested in investigating how such a phenomenon develops with the passage of time, as it is characterized at the beginning and the end of childhood, which factors influence the child's perception and those that influence the adult perception etc.

Points for Discussion

The first point that needs to be considered is that the cognitive approach has been, in recent decades, the area of psychology that has developed most in Europe and the United States. Surprisingly, however, the krowledge generated by this area has been sectorized, around the wor d. The result of this sectorization has created isolation in the relation of cognitive psychology with the other areas, generating losses of both sides.

Overcoming this impasse requires the differentiation between specialized competencies and sectoral competences, which do not necessarily have the same meaning: while the former is legitimate and useful for the progress of knowledge, the latter, in general, do not have this interdisciplinary sensitivity. The specialized competencies have a systematic concern within the investigations of the phenomena themselves, that is, they try to consider the relativistic character and theoretical-practical bias of the investigation proper to a given area.

The sectoral competences produce and treat knowledge in a circular way, closed in on itself. The proposal is not that the various areas of psychological science lose their specialty, but that this does not create the confinement and fragmentation of knowledge. The knowledge generated in each of these areas needs to be interchangeable without losing their specialized identity.

In search of more adequate and less simplistic explanations of human behavior, cognitive psychology has contributed to the understanding of phenomena of interest in other areas outside Psychology. Thus, a second point that deserves careful consideration is the question of transposing the theoretical results of cognitive research into praxis in other areas, such as educational, for example. The contribution of cognitive psychology to education is unquestionable, but this transposition requires an interdisciplinary action to adequately enable the passage of results from psychological research to pedagogical praxis.

Care should be taken with the aim of avoiding a reductionist and simplistic approach to theories and results of cognitive research within the school context, or an exclusively psychological approach to pedagogical problems.

A third aspect refers to the incomprehension between cognitive and Piagetian psychology. According to the above, it is essential to make a distinction between cognitive studies and Piagetian studies. The first step towards this is to seek a characterization of what is cognitive psychology since this incomprehension does not lie only between non-psychologists, but within psychology itself. The introductory disciplines of undergraduate courses could include in their program's reflections of this nature, thus preventing new generations of psychologists from incurring the same kind of misunderstanding. Apparently, incomprehension needs to be clarified within psychology itself.

Chapter 15 - First Impression

Is the First Impression So Important?

You do not need more than a minute to form a first impression of someone. I'm sure you've been through it sometime in your life. You know a person and quickly, without knowing very well why end up making an assessment about it based on your first impression.

Their looks, manners, gestures, voice ... small details that make up a cataloged image, one way or another. This may surprise you, but studies say that, in general, people are very good at these brief analyses that describe first impressions.

Be that as it may, we usually have little time not only to analyze others but also to make a good impression. How do you say "You never get a second chance to make a first impression"?

Why Do We Make an Impression So Quickly?

Psychologists claim that we do this analysis not in 30 seconds but in milliseconds. In just a sigh we know if a person is to our liking or not, whether it inspires confidence or not. Why does this occur? This is an aspect that has to do with the evolution of our species. An adaptive resource is very easy to understand.

If the person before us is judged as a threat or danger, our first reaction is to flee. People need to make instant assessments to make decisions right now. In a way, such seemingly rapid analyzes have a lot to do with our personality, our fears, and also with our needs.

It is true that we have our own experience of the instinctive - and almost irrational - the part that tells us immediately whether something is harmless or threatening, but our personal experience also counts a lot in these moments.

You may find an elegant and well-dressed person and can judge her as cramped and shallow; maybe this happens because you prefer a slightly more casual image because it gives you more intimacy and you remember your friends ... all the traits have a lot to do with our personality and our particular style. We could say that our brain is programmed to come to a quick conclusion with little information.

How Does the First Impression Work?

Every day we receive thousands of stimuli. We do not have time to process them or thoroughly analyze all this information. So how do we make decisions? Unconsciously. This is the reality; most of our decisions take us, quickly and unconsciously, to where our feelings, our memories, our experiences, our personality are stored ... the brain is working to organize the information into categories, and from there make very comparisons fast, and always with the help of our emotions.

Is not this person akin to someone from our past who has hurt us? Is the tone good? Do you have a smile as sincere as our father's, or is it as false as one of our neighbors?

Beware of the "Halo Effect"

The halo effect is a common cognitive bias. It has to do with the influence of our perceptions on our judgments of a person's qualities, from our first impression.

A clear example of the halo effect might be, for example, meeting a person who is physically attractive to us. When we see your beautiful image, we tend to think that your actions, your opinions, and your beliefs, will be as positive as your physical appearance.

Sometimes people make mistakes. The first impression has a direct effect, we cannot deny, but need not be decisive. We never know what lurks behind an image, and there may be no better adventure than finding out what lies behind an image.

First Impression: Only Half A Second Is Enough to Form It

According to a new study, only half a second - or a simple "hello" - is enough to draw conclusions about a person's personality and judge if it pleases him. And, according to the research, one does not necessarily have to be looking at the other to make that kind of judgment.

Researchers reached these conclusions after asking 320 people to report their impressions after listening to the recordings of different individuals saying hello. Volunteers should say what they felt about the voices based on ten criteria defined by the research - among them reliability and enthusiasm.

According to the researchers, most of the recordings caused the same reactions among the participants, and this judgment was set at only 300 to 500 milliseconds. One of the most considered characteristics for the volunteers was the confidence the voice conveyed - for the most part, men who raised their voices seemed more reliable, for example.

The team concluded that the tone of a person's voice when saying "hello" is able to immediately form the first impression someone will have of her. According to the researchers, this may be a reflection of the recent history of the human being, in which it has become increasingly important for survival to identify what it is possible to trust.

It is surprising that such small speeches can make such a definitive impression on a person, and moreover, that these impressions are the same in different listeners.

Chapter 16 - Using Your Body Language

How to Know and Read the Mind of People Through Their Gestures?

It is very interesting to know how you can read what the other person is transmitting you, sometimes unconscious by it, through the gestures of his body. It's true the body speaks. You can even experiment with your child, with a friend, a boyfriend, with someone who is by your side.

If you are not an actor, you can contradict yourself in what you are speaking by your gestures and the other person to detect and come to the conclusion that you are lying.

The most important instrument of the human being in his hands. There are many signs that they convey to us. Here's just one example: People when they want to be honest and sincere open their hands to the other person and say, "I did not do anything" or "I'm telling the truth."

The Power of The Outstretched Hand

It is the source of some of the most powerful body signals, whether in the transmission of commands or commands or in a simple handshake. The open hand, if properly displayed, gives the executor of the gesture unquestionable authority. Remember that the pointed index finger raises negative feelings in most listeners.

The Handshake

The diversity of information we can learn is incredible, the way we shake hands and how we are greeted at the hands of others. I'll get back to the subject.

The Secret of Laughter and Smiles - The Gestures Are Fantastic

Scientists are able to distinguish true smiles from false ones using the so-called FACS.

True smiles are unconsciously generated by the brain, which means that they are automatic. When you feel pleasure, some signs circulate through the part of your brain that processes emotion, causing the muscles of your mouth to move, your cheeks rise, your eyes narrow and your eyebrows droop slightly.

Have you ever heard of "mirror neurons"? What is most remarkable is that smiling at a person provokes a reciprocal and equal reaction, even when both smiles are false.

Attention to Signs with Arms

There are countless signs. Here we will remember that crossing your arms appreciably diminishes your credibility. It means putting a barrier between you and the other person. A strong message: "I am not willing, I do not accept, I do not go, etc. ..."

So, crossing your arms in front of your body is always seen as negative, and the message is both in the head of the recipient and in the person, who sends it. Even if you fold your arms because, say, you have back pain, the observer will unconsciously perceive you as a closed person to your ideas.

Signs by Look

It's like magic. How many times have you heard that the "eyes are the mirror of the soul"? What the pupils want to tell us. Reading through the gestures of the pupils.

The pupils bring very subtle messages, which often go unnoticed. However, they have their own language that can be deciphered. The most visible aspect is the dilation of the pupils, which automatically changes size according to the circumstances and without our intervention.

Usually, the pupils dilate when we see an interesting object and that we accept without hesitation, or in the penumbra when we have difficulty to see something. If lighting and visibility conditions are normal, dilation of the pupil is a sign of interest and attraction.

The opposite is also true. When we are faced with something we reject or feel afraid, the pupil's contract. The contracted pupils show hostility or bad mood, even if we are not looking directly at the object that displeases us.

The eyes move. They tell us a lot. Watch the movements. The movement of the eyes is continuous. Waking up or sleeping, there is always a movement. Something we can read / capture.

When the eyes move upward and lean to the right, the person is trying to imagine, describing, creativity.

If the movement is up and to the left, we activate the functions related to memories.

Looking down and to the right, we remember a feeling.

Now look down and to the left, we are talking to ourselves.

Small Examples of Non-Verbal Communication

Pay attention, study more, look for information. It is a subject that requires dedication, however, once you master it is very interesting.

Closed Eyes

It is more than likely that a person who keeps his eyes closed during a conversation wishes to protect himself from the world. It is important to note that this is not a sign of fear. Instead, it is an attempt to ward off an unwanted presence or thought. When the eyes are closed, you cannot see things around you, including you.

Hands on Your Mouth

You probably remember that reference in children. Children put their hands over their mouths when they do not want to talk about anything. Adults do it sometimes, too. A palm or fist over the mouth restricts the flow of words.

This action may also manifest in the form of a cough or sneezing.

Biting Your Glasses

A person who bites his glasses may need a little joy. That someone is probably worried about something. Biting things is a subconscious manifestation of the need to feel secure.

Face Projection

Physical gestures that call attention to the face are more often reserved for members of the opposite sex. A man who recognizes this body language would know that that is a great time to praise a woman about her appearance.

Rubbing the Chin

This usually happens when a person is making a decision. The eyes may be focused on an object or wandering in various directions. This is because the individual is probably thinking deeply and is not aware of what is happening around them.

Cross Arms

Everyone has seen a person with both arms crossed in the chest. There are individuals who comfort themselves in this position because they place a barrier between themselves and others that they find irritating or that cause some kind of discomfort. A person with folded arms is bothered by something.

Fixing by Appearance

A woman who wants to catch the eye of a man will perform in a desirable manner. She can straighten her back by projecting her breasts forward. She can cross her legs. A woman with her hands clasped below her waist is giving a clear signal of interest.

Lean Forward

People who like someone can connect subconsciously with them by leaning toward them. The legs often remain immobile, but the upper body protrudes forward.

Leaning Back

When a person leans back in his chair, it is a sign that he is tired of the conversation. It is quite possible that the subject involved in the conversation has caused some discomfort.

Foot Movement

This is usually seen only in children. It's a sign that something made the child anxious or worried.

Rubbing Hands

It is said that the hands reflect a person's thoughts. When someone rubs both hands, it is a sign that the person is feeling excited or happy. This happens when there is a good expectation about the future.

"Gloved" Handshake

A person using the second hand to hold the wrist during a handshake demonstrates that it can be trusted.

Handshake with The Palm Facing the Ceiling

A handshake with one palm under the person's hand and the other at the top is a demonstration of sympathy. However, this is only valid if the upper hand is offered immediately. When the upper hand is offered as a delayed reaction, it is a sign of dominance.

Handshake with Palm Facing Down

The act of holding a person's hand in their hands and placing it under their palm communicates a desire to help.

Handshake Accompanied by A Touch

Sometimes people touch the other person's elbow, arm or back while shaking hands. This is an invasion of private space and indicates a lack of fellowship. When this touch is near the trunk, it is an even stronger sign that one needs companionship.

Trimming the Tie

The meaning of this gesture may vary according to the situation. A man who does this in the presence of a woman is probably attracted to her. This gesture can also indicate a level of discomfort. A third possibility is that the person has just told a lie and is preparing to escape the current situation.

Look for Hair Strands That Do Not Exist

This gesture is a clear demonstration of displacement. Often expresses a mute disagreement, that is, that the other person does not want to explain.

Feet on The Table

This gesture is associated with some things. It could be a simple lack of education, a sense of disrespect or demonstration of mastery. Individuals who feel comfortable in this position should only stay in their own homes.

Visual Contact

The eyes are the best communication tools. A person's emotions and feelings appear clearly through the eyes. Pupils often dilate when the person is in the presence of a romantic attraction. It has also been observed that the pupil's contract when a person is angry.

Conclusion

Thank you for making it through to the end of *How to Analyze People*, let's hope it was informative and able to provide you with all of the tools you need to achieve your goals whatever they may be.

Here are a few points to summarize:

It is not very realistic to expect that most of us will develop the kind of extra-sensory perception that will make us mind readers. However, all people can learn to identify the non-verbal clues that others demonstrate every day. These psychological tips will make you understand people perfectly in no time.

Most of the time we do not stop to think about the language of our body, what we transmit in non-verbal communication. It is even more important than the words we use, gestures, posture and facial expression reveal more than we can suppose or intend to demonstrate. To have control of these movements is to be able to pass the message of the emotions and thoughts in a balanced way, reinforcing the words with the gestures. Research indicates that only

7% of our communication is word-based. The body language is responsible for another 55% and the tone of voice for 38%.

A negative body language can convey weakness, insecurity. And we do not want our interlocutor to have that impression. Having the knowledge and mastery of our body makes a lot of difference in personal and professional relationships from the moment we recognize their power. A correct and upright posture requires training and corrections until you reach perfection. Sitting in the right way according to the environment, without exposing yourself too much, demonstrates education. Standing without arms crossed or hands in pockets conveys confidence and security. Walking elegantly, even with very high heels, without much movement in the hips and without looking at the ground, projects positivity. The body should always be moved smoothly, without sudden movements or drama.

Accelerated or aggressive rhythm generates a sense of stress and lack of confidence. Carrying your hand over your mouth while talking or looking away from the caller gives the impression of lying. The look, then, is extremely revealing. No matter how hard we try to hide our emotions, it shows the truth of our feelings. How many times do we say one thing believing another? Those who pay attention to their eyes will realize how much truthfulness there is in words. An unfocused look can be confusing as if you are looking for a mental image for support. The famous twist of eyes denotes irritation and contempt. To contact the forehead means tension, doubt or nervousness, a very negative point. Crossing one's arms away from the others, representing the imposition of a physical barrier, that is, no opening as to what is being said. On the plus side, a firm handshake demonstrates confidence. Speaking calmly, articulating the words well and maintaining tranquility, conveys credibility. Who believes in someone who does not express himself correctly, speaks in a fiddly way, without coherence of thoughts?

Knowledge and mastery of body language techniques add value to our relationships in any environment. Analyzing and learning how to deal with our gestural is a differential in social relations, there is no denying.

Finally, if you found this book useful in any way, a review on Amazon is always appreciated!